THE NATURALIST IN LONDON

In the same series

published

THE NATURALIST IN CENTRAL SOUTHERN
ENGLAND
(Hampshire, Berkshire, Wiltshire, Dorset and Somerset)
by Derrick Knowlton

THE NATURALIST IN DEVON AND CORNWALL
by Roger Burrows

THE NATURALIST IN THE ISLE OF MAN
by Larch S. Garrad

THE NATURALIST IN LAKELAND
by Eric Hardy

THE NATURALIST IN MAJORCA
by James D. Parrack

THE NATURALIST IN WALES
by R. M. Lockley

THE NATURALIST IN SOUTH-EAST ENGLAND
(Kent, Surrey and Sussex)
by S. A. Manning

THE REGIONAL NATURALIST

THE NATURALIST IN

London

JOHN A. BURTON

DAVID & CHARLES

NEWTON ABBOT LONDON
NORTH POMFRET (VT) VANCOUVER

ISBN 0 7153 6215 1

Library of Congress Catalog Card Number 74-78247

Set in 12 on 13 point Bembo
and printed in Great Britain
by Latimer Trend & Company Ltd Plymouth
for David & Charles (Holdings) Limited
South Devon House Newton Abbot Devon

Published in the United States of America
by David & Charles Inc
North Pomfret Vermont 05053 USA

Published in Canada
by Douglas David & Charles Limited
3645 McKechnie Drive West Vancouver BC

Contents

List of Illustrations

IN TEXT

Preface

THIS BOOK IS intended primarily for the naturalist visiting London for a limited period of time, and I have tried to give as wide a selection of places worth a visit as possible. Inevitably certain biases have arisen, but I have tried to keep them to a minimum and have attempted to select typical representatives of the most important and most interesting habitats to be found in and around the capital. I became very conscious of having mentioned rather more localities south of the Thames than north of it. I tried to remedy this, feeling that it must be due to the fact that I myself have always lived in the south but, in fact, I found that there really are more parks and open spaces there, due no doubt to the fact that it was 'developed' later than the north. I have given prominence to birds, since birdwatchers are easily the most numerous species of naturalist.

If after reading this book you believe that London is not a barren wasteland, devoid of wildlife, then I shall rest happy. I am convinced that in the next few years a new outlook will arise. All too often city-dwelling naturalists—and most naturalists spend a good deal of their lives in cities—spend their time bewailing the loss of this or that species or looking for rarities and vagrants. The fact that a few dozen species of animals and plants have become extinct does not surprise me nearly as much as the fact that some have not only survived, but have adapted to the newly created environments so well as to actually benefit from man's activities. And yet these are the species generally ignored by field naturalists. Starlings, cockroaches, fleas, rats, sparrows, pigeons, cats and dogs—all these and many more go to make up the fauna of the city. They are all abundant

9

and widespread, but I wonder how much notice is taken of them each time the hundreds of naturalists living in London venture forth. Yet there is a growing awareness of our immediate environment. Already naturalists are sufficiently awake to be as likely to visit a sewage farm, rubbish tip, power station or dock, as anywhere truly rural.

The future of London's natural wildlife is a vital question. When Richard Fitter wrote his classic *London's Natural History* in 1945, the editors in their preface made the somewhat pessimistic comment that 'Mr. Fitter's book makes somewhat gloomy reading, for the progressive biological sterilisation of London is a sad history.' In actual fact the author's painstaking detailing of all the changes that have taken place in London, while pointing out the losses, draws attention to gains which have more than compensated. The pessimistic attitude probably dates back to the early naturalist writers on London, one of the most prolific of whom was W. H. Hudson. Anyone delving into the history of London's birds becomes involved with the writings of Hudson. An ardent protectionist, he devoted much of his time to promoting the early bird protection bills and to pamphleteering, yet his writing is full of despondency about the future. In *Birds of London* he writes, '1 Many species formerly resident throughout the year in London have quite died out. 2 Some resident species are reduced to small remnants and are confined to one or to a very few spots. 3 Several other species formerly common have greatly decreased in numbers. 4 The decrease has been in most, but not all, of the old residents.' Hudson does end on a slightly more optimistic note when he states that '5 At the same time that some of the old residents have been decreasing or dying out, a few other species have come in from the outside and have greatly increased.'

All five of Hudson's comments are, broadly speaking, still true. The decrease in some species continues while other species increase and even colonise new areas. Hudson would doubtless be amazed at some of the birds he would encounter now. Who, at the turn of the century, would have predicted that London would be the home for some of the largest breeding populations of black redstarts or little ringed plovers in Great Britain; or that 250,000 gulls would be roosting on the reservoirs? The fortunes of the dabchick were rising at the turn of the century, but they have since declined. The tawny owl was described by J. E. Harting in his classic *Birds of Middlesex* (1866) as being rare and only a handful of occurrences are recorded for the previous half century. Although more often noted by the end of the century when Hudson was writing, the only inner London park he recorded it from was Kensington Gardens. David Montier, writing in 1968, found tawny owls widely distributed in London, being completely absent only from totally urbanised areas. The important conclusion to draw from the above is that London is constantly changing, probably far more than does a so-called 'natural' habitat. The direction these changes take is often interesting, surprising, but rarely predictable.

Ultimately natural history, conservation and ecology all converge on one factor—human populations. In the few thousand years that 'civilised' man has been with us he has devastated the landscape; within the next few decades most of the population of the British Isles (and the rest of the world for that matter) will be living in towns. It is my firm belief that naturalists will be wasting their time if they devote their energies entirely to County Naturalists' Trusts, World Wildlife Fund, Royal Society for the Protection of Birds and other such worthy causes. Dr Paul R. Ehrlich, a prolific writer on the problem, summarises the situation neatly when he states:

> In spite of all the efforts of conservationists, all the propaganda, all the eloquent writing, all the beautiful pictures, the conservation battle is presently being lost. In my years of interest in this question I've come to the conclusion that it is being lost for two powerful reasons. The first, of course, is that nothing 'undeveloped' can long stand in the face of the population explosion. The second is that most people clearly don't give a damn. They've never heard of the California condor and would share no tears if it became extinct. Indeed many people would compete for the privilege of shooting the last one.

It is the duty of every naturalist to be concerned about the environment as a whole, to read the works of Paul Ehrlich, Edward Goldsmith and the many others, showing the devastating effects that the rising population is having on the world.

CHAPTER ONE

Introduction

Definition of London—Historical growth—
Climate today

DEFINITION OF LONDON

LONDON IS ONE of the largest conurbations in the world and one
of the most difficult areas to define satisfactorily. Using the
names of administrative counties is of little help for, unfortunately, county boundaries are liable to change. The cities of
Westminster and London both used to fall within the county of
Middlesex, and the other counties which could be considered as
having some part in London were Essex, Kent, Surrey and, to
a lesser extent, Hertfordshire. But only recently in a programme
of reorganisation the former London County extended its boundaries to become Greater London. In the process Middlesex was
engulfed, most of it being incorporated into Greater London,
but some parts coming under Surrey. Minor changes in the
county borders often take place and so most naturalists use the
Watsonian vice-county boundaries for recording purposes, since
these are stable and allow comparisons to be made regardless of
the date of the observations.

Defining the actual limits of London's growth is difficult too—
what is London today may have been green fields and woods a
decade ago, and what are green fields and woods today may be
part of the suburban sprawl within the next decade. The London
Natural History Society, one of the largest and most active
groups of naturalists in the London area, defines London for
recording purposes as anywhere within a twenty-mile radius of

St Paul's Cathedral. This area obviously includes a considerable amount of truly rural countryside.

For the purposes of this book, any reference to present-day London is to London in its loosest sense, ie meaning the conurbation composed of Greater London and some of the adjacent boroughs. Any references to counties are to the Watsonian counties, not the present-day administrative areas.

HISTORICAL GROWTH

In order to understand the natural history of the metropolis and its environs it is necessary to know a little about London's history and how the environment has changed over the centuries. Little is known of London before the coming of the Romans but probably some sort of settlement was already well established. There have been many finds dating from Neolithic and Bronze Age times along the Thames, from Mortlake, Battersea and several other sites, indicating a series of settlements alongside the river. Some discoveries, such as the shield found in the Thames near Battersea and now in the British Museum, are spectacular and beautiful. The marshes beside the Thames undoubtedly teemed with wildlife, providing an ample food supply. As late as Tudor times spoonbills were to nest in the marshes near Fulham Palace.

Although Julius Caesar made a brief visit to Britain in 55 BC, it was not until nearly a century later that Britain was invaded and subjugated. Between AD 43 and 50 Aulus Plautus brought most of Britain more or less under control and it was during the first couple of decades of the Roman occupation that Londinium was built on two low hills just north of the Thames where St Paul's Cathedral and the Bank of England now stand. Doubtless the site had been occupied by earlier inhabitants of the region, as Iron Age remains, and those from earlier periods, have been found in and around London. During the Roman occupation London's first bridge was erected, probably slightly downstream from today's London Bridge. This bridge, and its successors, was to remain the only permanent link with the southern bank of the Thames, apart from ferries and fords, until 1750 when Westminster Bridge was built. Ferries and fords were no doubt common enough, but all that time the land south of the Thames was relatively cut off from London. However, the Thames just above Westminster even today is as little as four feet deep in mid channel, at a spring tide; were it not for the pot-holes, one might be able to wade across.

It is probable that some of the first embankments along the Thames were built by the Romans—a process which has continued ever since, the Thames being forced into an ever-narrowing channel. Another feature of the Thames in Roman times was that the tides probably reached no further than London Bridge or Westminster, nowadays they reach the first lock at Teddington. This is connected with the general subsidence of the east coast of England and there is a consequent danger of severe flooding occurring in London. Floods have occurred on several occasions and although barrages and other protective measures have been talked about for many years, parts of London are still without any adequate protection against an abnormal tide.

At some time during the second century AD the Romans built the city wall, which enclosed an area of some 320 acres. The wall ran from what was later to become the Tower of London, north and westwards in an arc and back to Blackfriars. The wall was maintained throughout the Middle Ages and the names of the gates are commemorated in place names: Aldgate, Bishopsgate, Moorgate, Cripplegate, Aldersgate, Newgate and Ludgate. Many of the remains of the ancient city, found during building works and by archaeologists, are displayed in the Guildhall and London Museums.

After the departure of the Romans, London declined. The conquering waves of Saxons, Jutes and Angles were not accustomed to urban life, and it is quite probable that the population decreased during this period. By the ninth century Alfred the Great was attempting to unify southern England and make a stand against the dreaded Viking marauders who had plundered

London on several occasions. After this period of unrest London began to flourish once more, and Edward the Confessor built a palace outside the city at Westminster and also started rebuilding the abbey there. William the Conqueror, the first king to be crowned in the abbey, gave London its first charter.

In the year of William's death one of the many fires, which have devastated London periodically, destroyed a large part of the city including St Paul's Cathedral. The next few decades saw the rebuilding of the cathedral and extension to the fortification of the Tower of London. Another fire in 1136 severely damaged London Bridge and, between 1176 and 1209, the bridge which was to become one of the wonders of medieval Europe, was built. There were houses, shops and even a chapel on the bridge, and the nineteen supporting arches created such a strong current that 'shooting' the bridge was considered a great skill. This bridge was finally demolished in 1830.

London was expanding rapidly and the suburbs were beginning to spread outside the city walls, but the population in the thirteenth century was probably still less than 50,000. By Elizabeth I's reign London was one of the most important, busiest and wealthiest cities in the world, a flourishing centre of commerce and culture. The spread of the suburbs was so rapid that in 1580 a royal edict forbade building within three miles of the city walls. At about the same time the south bank suburbs began to expand rapidly, centred on Southwark. By 1600 the population was somewhere in the region of 150,000.

The Great Fire of London in 1666 cleared the city after the last and most destructive of the plagues which periodically ravaged Europe. The fire destroyed some five-sixths of the city: 13,000 dwellings and 89 churches as well as many important public buildings, including St Paul's Cathedral. This was rebuilt from 1675 to 1710 and plans were made for a city which would have been years in advance of its time, but piecemeal building foiled the grandiose plans of the architects and London began to take the form in which we ourselves know it. The Industrial Revolution started the expansion of London into the vast sprawl

Page 17 (*above*) A bird's eye view of London near the Strand—but to a bird or plant probably not much different from a rocky cliff; (*below*) the River Thames. Slowly becoming cleaner, fish have returned and ducks winter on the lower reaches

The classic example of industrial melanism, the peppered moth *Biston betilaria*.
The rural form is pale and is well camouflaged against a lichenous tree (*left*); the black form, which is well camouflaged against sooty trees (*right*), is as obvious against a lichenous tree as the pale form is on a sooty tree

that it is today. In 1836 the first train left a London terminus and the establishment of passenger services accelerated the pushing out of the suburbs at an almost breakneck pace. The Great War had relatively little effect on London, but World War II devastated the City. The blitz of London in 1941, often known as the Second Great Fire of London, destroyed large areas, the last of which have only recently been rebuilt. The devastation provided naturalists with a unique chance to study wildlife under near-natural conditions in the heart of the city.

The last two decades have seen some of the most rapid and drastic changes of all. London has risen higher than ever before; tall blocks of flats and offices loom up everywhere, completely altering the skyline. Flyovers and underpasses convey streams of traffic up to six lanes wide, ever faster. The atmosphere is laden with exhaust fumes and smoke. Daylight seems a long way up; the noise is deafening; the glare of street lights keeps a permanent glow in the sky.

In recent years the suburbs of London have extended further and further out, particularly along the arterial roads, so that it seems they are almost continuous from London to Brighton along the A23. Fortunately for Londoners, the Town & Country Planning Act has managed to halt the encroachment of the suburbs on the countryside surrounding London and to preserve a 'green belt'. Even in the distant past there were open spaces in the centre of London for the recreation of its inhabitants; today few cities of a comparable size can boast as many parks, commons, woods and gardens. Many open spaces such as St James's Park, Richmond Park, and Kensington Gardens were at one time the property of the monarchy, while others such as Wimbledon and Streatham Commons, Hampstead Heath and Blackheath are the commonlands which remained after the enclosures of the sixteenth century onwards. Yet others such as Epping Forest and Farthing Down were purchased with the express idea of providing recreational areas for Londoners.

CLIMATE TODAY

T. J. Chandler writing on the climate of London in 1965 estimated that atmospheric pollution was costing Londoners about £50 million each year, without taking into account the cost to health and other similar factors which are difficult to value. In recent years there has been some effort to reduce such pollution in London and smoke emissions have indeed been reduced. It was largely smoke which produced the famous pea-soup fogs such as the 'smog' of December 1952 which killed about 4,000 people, and the last major smog was in 1962, when only about 340 people died. Soot blocks the pores of plants; sulphur dioxide, the other main pollutant in London's atmosphere, attacks the cells of mesophyll of plants and will eventually kill them; the general effect of the atmospheric pollution is to reduce the number of hours of sunlight reaching street level—in mid-winter there may be one to two hours difference between London and the surrounding countryside.

The sheer size and density of London is another factor giving it a climate quite different from its environs. Measurements taken over a thirty-year period showed that central London had a mean annual temperature of $11°$ C ($51.8°$ F), whereas the temperature in the countryside surrounding London was $9.6°$ C ($49.2°$ F)—a difference of $1.4°$ C. The average annual rainfall for the period 1916 to 1950 was normally over 25in per year on the South Downs and over 30in per year on the North Downs, whereas in central London it was usually less than 25in. In contrast therefore to the disadvantages of the soot and grime of the city, there is a genuine advantage to be gained by living in central London; it is definitely warmer and drier than the surrounding districts.

CHAPTER TWO

Among the buildings of central London

Street level and below—Colonisation of bombed sites—
Birds—Flora—Nature indoors—Some rarities

VERY FEW PEOPLE would think of the buildings of central London, ie the cities of Westminster and London, the West End and as far east as the docks, as a naturalist's haven. However, a surprising variety of wildlife does exist there in spite of the interference and pollution, while below street level often spectacular discoveries illustrate the natural history of past ages.

STREET LEVEL AND BELOW

An ecologist wishing to understand in detail a certain habitat will, at some point or other, have to examine the surface geostructure of that area. In the case of major built-up centres such as London this is particularly interesting. Although small differences may be detected in the geo-structure of various towns and cities they have many features in common: vast quantities of brick, mortar, concrete, tarmac, slate, terracotta, glass and miscellaneous natural stones from all over the world. These latter stones make an absorbing study in themselves; since buildings of different periods tended to be constructed of different stone as fashion and availability dictated. And beneath the buildings and tarmac of London's streets are strata composed of the remains of previous occupants of the city, dating back to Roman times, and even beyond. In some places the depth of evidence of Roman occupation is over twenty feet below street level.

Examination of the fossil strata beneath London is difficult due to its inaccessibility, but when foundations for buildings are being excavated, interesting discoveries are sometimes made. In 1731, an elephant's tooth was found beneath Pall Mall. From time to time further remains have come to light, but it was not until 1959 that any systematic collection was made. In that year, during the digging of the foundations for Uganda House on the south side of Trafalgar Square, scientists made a detailed study of the exposed strata. Their finds captured public imagination, showing as they did that elephant, hippopotamus and aurochs all lived in the area. The elephant was a large now extinct species, the straight-tusked. There were also numerous other fossils, including many plant remains which allowed an analysis of the ecology of the habitat and climate. It appears that in the late Pleistocene Period the climate of central London was much warmer, with lush vegetation bordering the slow-moving river. This particular site has disappeared but whenever deep foundations are constructed, sewers laid or similar construction work carried out, it is always well worth examining the spoil heaps for fossil remains.

Most of north London and part of south London is built on the Lower Eocene London Clay and therefore many of the building operations excavate this. In order to study this sub-soil, it is necessary to record as accurately as possible the precise location of the excavation and, if possible, depths and measurements of the section. Samples of clay of at least 25lb should be removed, slowly baked dry in an oven, soaked with water, stirred into a slurry and wet sieved to recover the fossils.

A naturalist in the heart of London could do worse than examine its soil for living creatures. Even in central London soil mites, earthworms, nematodes and pseudoscorpions have been found.

The overall effect of the mass known as London must, to wildlife, look remarkably similar to a series of rocky cliffs and gorges. What then prevents London from being taken over by wildlife? The answers are disturbance and pollution. Disturbance is by far the most important factor, except in areas of excessive pollution. Wherever disturbance is absent wildlife usually manages to gain a foothold. It has often been argued that the high level of atmospheric pollution is the main factor limiting the amount of life in cities but actual observations reveal that, very often, it is the degree of disturbance which controls the number and variety of living things. Normally mosses, ferns and grasses are scraped from any crevices in which they have managed to gain a hold, and it is very difficult to observe a city such as London under undisturbed conditions. The nearest approach to these conditions probably occurred during and immediately after World War II, when the blitz of London left large districts of the city in a state of collapse and, in many places, the crumbling buildings were merely levelled or the loose rubble removed. Almost at once nature's colonisation of the bombed sites began.

COLONISATION OF BOMBED SITES

To wildlife the bombed sites were much the same as the rest of London with one big difference, no one tidied or cleared away plants; for once man, usually so tidy, was content to let nature take over the buildings or their remains. Many plants and animals established themselves so well that even after the disappearance of the devastated areas they managed to survive in central London. Thus this war-produced habitat is worth mentioning in some detail.

The abundance of plant life which so soon invaded the bombed sites and created a green oasis in the heart of London was a source of food for a wide variety of insects, many of which drifted into the city on the same winds as the plant seeds. Many insects were unable to stand the high level of soot pollution but, like the plants, there are many species which are very robust and which were capable of taking full advantage of the newly created habitat. The rosebay willow herb (see page 35) is a favourite food of the beautiful crimson-pink elephant hawk moth and wherever rosebay is found it is possible that these moths, or their caterpillars, will be near. Some species of moths have even changed their colour to suit the urban environment: the peppered moth was originally a whitish moth but over the years a black, or melanistic, form has become increasingly abundant. This is because the trees on which it lives have become increasingly darkened with soot deposits and a dark insect form is less obvious to predators. Other moths and butterflies found their way into London as well as flies, wasps and various other kinds of insects, including a species of grasshopper which was probably imported in the same manner as the grasses—in a horse's nosebag.

Although free from man's interference, in one particular sense the bombed sites were a harsh environment. They were very arid as bricks and concrete do not retain moisture efficiently, and with lack of shade from overshadowing buildings the temperature in the open spaces of rubble was high. The effect of this was that by August many of the plants were shrivelling up, and the insects competing for food had a struggle for survival. Only plant and animal species which could complete their life cycle before the 'drought' could survive such conditions.

The abundance of insect and plant life soon attracted birds, as they are amongst the most mobile of animals. During the early stages of colonisation, bombing was still in progress and knowledge of the natural history is thus somewhat sketchy, but undoubtedly the first birds to take advantage of the newly created habitat were the ubiquitous house sparrows and feral pigeons. Many migrants such as goldfinches visited the bombed sites, feeding on the abundant supply of seeds, and it is probable that some of the berry-bearing plants such as hawthorn, mountain ash and elder, originated from seeds in the droppings of blackbirds and thrushes. Kestrels were already to be found in small numbers in built-up parts of London and were not slow to move into the bombed sites, preying largely on sparrows.

The most spectacular species of bird to colonise the blitzed areas was the black redstart, a prettily plumaged bird related to the chats and robins and feeding largely on insects. The male black redstart is slate-grey above, paler on the underside, with a bright rufous tail. The female is more drab. Superficially the slate-grey colours of the black redstart would seem to be some sort of protective colouration as camouflage on the soot-encrusted buildings of the city. This is not so, but may be a happy coincidence.

During the nineteenth century the black redstart was almost unknown in this country, with only one or two isolated breeding records and the occasional bird seen on passage, but on the mainland of Europe they were expanding their range. During the first decades of the twentieth century they began to occur in England with increasing frequency, first breeding in 1923 and from 1927 onwards breeding in London around Wembley, though they are still one of Britain's rarest breeding birds. In 1942 when they appeared on the bombed sites, there began one of the most fascinating chapters in the story of London's bird life.

By the end of the war the colony of black redstarts on the Cripplegate bombed sites was well established. The male black redstarts arrived towards the end of March, followed by the females in early April. The males soon established a territory which they proclaimed to all contenders by singing from the tops of buildings. They had an abundance of nest sites, which varied in height from a cellar below ground to six or seven storeys up, and were usually situated in crevices or holes in broken masonry. The large numbers of insects on the bombed sites provided adult birds and their young with readily available food.

Black redstarts are ready parents. The four or five eggs hatch early in June but, if the first clutch or young are accidentally destroyed, or if the young are successfully reared early enough, the birds often lay a second clutch of eggs. In late September or early October they begin to migrate southwards, though the

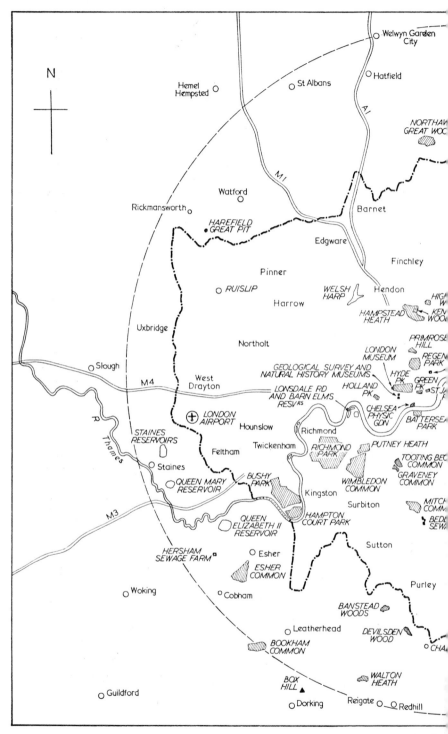

N

Welwyn Garden City

Hemel Hempsted

St Albans

Hatfield

NORTHAW GREAT WOO

Watford

Rickmansworth

Barnet

HAREFIELD GREAT PIT

Edgware

Finchley

Pinner

Hendon

RUISLIP

WELSH HARP

HIGH W

Harrow

KEN WOO

HAMPSTEAD HEATH

Uxbridge

Northolt

PRIMROSE HILL

LONDON MUSEUM

REGEN PARK

Slough

GEOLOGICAL SURVEY AND NATURAL HISTORY MUSEUMS

M4

West Drayton

HYDE PK

GREEN PK

ST J

LONSDALE RD AND BARN ELMS RESV^RS

HOLLAND PK

R Thames

BATTERSE PARK

CHELSEA PHYSIC GDN

LONDON AIRPORT

Hounslow

Richmond

STAINES RESERVOIRS

RICHMOND PARK

PUTNEY HEATH

Feltham

Twickenham

TOOTING BEC COMMON

Staines

WIMBLEDON COMMON

GRAVENEY COMMON

BUSHY PARK

Kingston

QUEEN MARY RESERVOIR

Surbiton

MITC COMM

M3

BED SEW

QUEEN ELIZABETH II RESERVOIR

HAMPTON COURT PARK

Sutton

HERSHAM SEWAGE FARM

Esher

Purley

Woking

ESHER COMMON

Cobham

BANSTEAD WOODS

Leatherhead

DEVILSDEN WOOD

BOOKHAM COMMON

CHA

WALTON HEATH

Guildford

BOX HILL ▲

Reigate

Redhill

Dorking

Londor

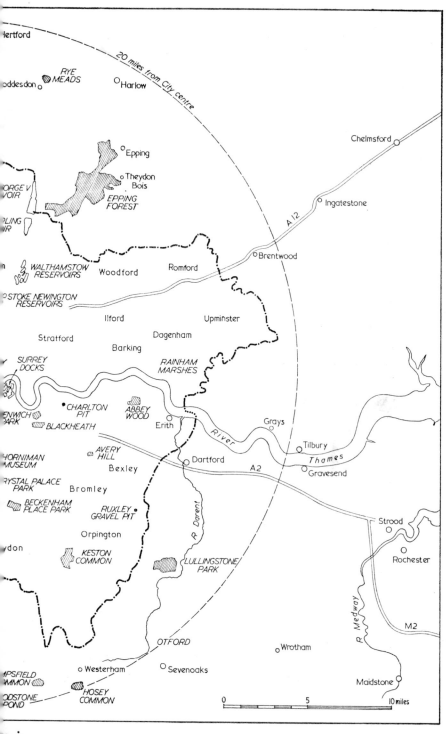

environs

young will have dispersed sometime earlier. Not all the birds move away and there are many instances of black redstarts wintering in London and other parts of England.

One of the most interesting and mysterious features of the black redstarts' colonisation of London is why they chose the centre. This is a question which is still unanswered. Black redstarts have in recent years bred in many other places in and around London, but have never reached the density that the bombed site populations reached. The explanation as to why they bred on the bombed sites is simple enough: it was an area with relatively little disturbance and an abundant supply of food and nest sites. But the question remains as to why they chose the centre in the first place; there are plenty of superficially similar habitats elsewhere.

With the redevelopment of the bombed sites fewer and fewer black redstarts were able to nest in central London. By the late 1960s there were only one or two pairs left though in 1970, when almost all the bombed sites had been rebuilt, males were found singing in Cripplegate and the Barbican. At the time of writing most of the breeding haunts of the black redstarts are away from central London, in industrial areas (see page 50).

BIRDS

Although the bombed sites have disappeared, another similar habitat still exists in the 'temporary industrial sites' created when areas are cleared for rebuilding. Very often the ruins and rubble are left vacant for several months, or even years, and the wildlife starts to invade. These temporary sites often attract a surprising variety of birds: goldfinches, greenfinches and chaffinches will often be seen feeding on plant seeds in autumn, and some birds will stay to nest if conditions are right. One of the most surprising observations of all was the successful breeding, in 1970, of two pairs of yellow wagtails on a small area of waste ground next to Vauxhall Bridge. Yellow wagtails are birds normally associated with marshes and water meadows, yet here, opposite the Tate Gallery and next to the near-opaque waters of the Thames and the deafening din of the construction site of London's latest underground railway, they raised their youngsters. The greatest surprise was yet to come however, when, in 1971, not only yellow wagtails but also a pair of little ringed plovers nested in the site of the old Surrey Docks. Another striking bird which regularly breeds in the city centre is the pied wagtail which may be encountered almost anywhere in London.

Other prominent birds are the London pigeons—the feral descendants of rock doves domesticated for eating or racing. The buildings of London are similar to their original breeding haunts on rocky cliffs, and they have bred prolifically. Office workers and tourists feed them, but it is a great pity that so few naturalists take any notice of them. They are one of the easiest birds to study in London and yet there is probably less known about these pigeons than about any other bird in the city. If a bird report mentions them at all it is usually full of generalisations. Being large and individually plumaged, they would lend themselves to detailed population studies.

The central London starlings have received more attention. Their flight-lines were carefully mapped over twenty years ago, and ringing studies showed that the starlings roosting around Trafalgar Square are gathered from a circle fifteen to eighteen miles out from the centre. Dusk in Trafalgar Square in late autumn is extremely impressive as thousands of starlings come in, arriving in flocks of several hundred, wheeling around Nelson atop of his column, land and squabble and wheel around again. The starlings form these flocks at various points on their flight-lines. By the time it is dark most of the birds will be settled on ledges, creating a problem for anyone who is trying to keep a building clean. All manner of cunning devices have been tried in order to discourage starlings from roosting on a particular site, but as yet there is no cheap and effective way of prevention.

The urban roosting of starlings is a fairly recent development. Until the beginning of the nineteenth century the starling was rare in the west of England, Wales, Scotland and Ireland. By

1875 the first town roost of starlings was noted in Glasgow and by the turn of the century they were beginning to roost in London. The London starling roost is one of the largest in Britain together with those of Bristol, Birmingham and Newcastle, all of which number between 10,000 and 15,000 birds. Only those of Bradford and Glasgow number more than 50,000 birds. The urban roosts are, in the main, drawn from resident birds—few winter visitors join them. The population of starlings in Britain at the beginning of the breeding season has been estimated at about 7 million, but in winter they are joined by some 40 million continental birds.

In comparatively recent years a rather surprising new member, the kestrel, has joined the avifauna of central London. Although there are probably fewer now than there were just after the war, it is still quite a common sight to see a kestrel hovering over almost any part of London. A pair which achieved considerable fame and publicity in the press, on television and in the cinema, nested for several years in the Langham Hotel, opposite the BBC building. The food of the kestrel in London contains a very high proportion of sparrows, a species which has in fact declined considerably in London, particularly in the centre. The reason for this is that the horse has disappeared from London's streets and with it the sparrow's food supply.

It is interesting to speculate on the future of the peregrine falcon, a species which has unfortunately recently suffered a catastrophic decline in numbers. In the years after World War II peregrines were occasionally seen in London and it is quite feasible that eventually they may settle and nest. The buildings of the city provide nest sites for the descendants of rock doves and these, together with starlings, are often one of the main food items of peregrines. In North America peregrines were frequently recorded in cities; one pair nesting regularly in Manhattan, New York, between 1943 and 1953. Unfortunately the peregrine population, not only in Britain, but over much of its range, has been reduced to a dangerously low level, largely due to the accumulative effect of pesticides such as DDT. If the population recouperates in the future it is quite possible that one day peregrine falcons will nest once more on St Paul's Cathedral.

FLORA

Although at first sight a barren waste of concrete, upon closer examination more and more green may be found in the city— trees growing in odd corners and small squares hidden in side streets. The trees found in central London are interesting, if only on the grounds of the strange mixture of species. In Bloomsbury and other parts of London the Chinese 'tree of heaven' grows alongside more familiar species such as sycamore and horse chestnut. But the most famous tree of all is the London plane. This is a hybrid produced from exotic species introduced into England over 300 years ago. Much of the London plane's success is due to the fact that the bark is shed periodically, and with it all the accumulation of soot and grime which has been deposited from the atmosphere. When the almost black soot-laden bark is shed, revealing the new yellowish bark beneath, it gives the plane trees their characteristic piebald appearance. In contrast to the plane trees, coniferous trees are conspicuously absent from central London. They easily succumb to the high level of atmospheric pollution—to such an extent that the conifers in the Royal Botanic Garden, as far out as Kew, had to be moved to purer air in Surrey.

From time to time in the squares and odd corners, various fruit trees spring up, remnants of an office worker's lunch. Apples, pears and cherries are common and other more exotic species such as figs and oranges have been recorded.

Around the built-up centre of London lie the suburbs with their intensely cultivated gardens. It is not surprising that some of these garden plants have found their way into the heart of the city. Railway embankments are good sites for unusual plants. The Himalayan balsam (*Impatiens glandulifera*) is a pretty garden escape which has been found on railway embankments near Paddington, and by the Regent's Canal at Islington.

Several of the plants which are so closely associated with London as to be considered characteristic are, in fact, introduced species. The most famous of these is the London rocket (*Sisymbrium irio*), so called because it first appeared in great numbers after the Great Fire of London in 1666. Since then it has declined drastically and is now a rarity, turning up sporadically in odd parts of central London and still to be found near the Tower of London. After the second great fire of London, the blitz of 1941, another plant sprang up in profusion. This was the rosebay willow herb (*Chamaenerion angustifolium*). In the nineteenth century it was a rarity but by the end of World War II it was probably the commonest plant in central London, its brilliant mauve adding a splash of colour to almost every bombed site. The broad-leaved willow herb (*Epilobium montanum*) and the great hairy willow herb (*E. hirsutum*) are also quite widespread in central London but have never become as abundant as the rosebay.

Another group of flowering plants characteristic of central London are the ragworts (*Senecio*). The common groundsel (*S. vulgaris*) is known to all gardeners as a prolific and rapidly spreading weed, but the so-called Oxford ragwort (*S. squalidus*), an introduced species, is even more successful in many parts of London. Its name is derived from its origin in Britain—the Botanic Gardens in Oxford, from which it escaped at the end of the eighteenth century. Its initial spread, largely along railway lines, was slow and it did not arrive in London until the 1860s. Since then it has established itself as one of the city's characteristic plants. Originally the Oxford ragwort was found on arid, volcanic mountains in Sicily. The buildings of London provide a similar habitat.

These plants, and many others, manage to grow in most precarious positions, such as cracks in the roof of an office block where soot and pigeon-droppings accumulate, retain moisture and form a poor soil in which a seed can take root. In the shady depths between office blocks bracken often takes root. But these plants only rarely mature; they either wither away or someone 'tidies' them.

NATURE INDOORS

Probably the most fascinating aspect of urban natural history is the world of nature indoors. In the basements and cellars of the centre of London live black rats, brown rats, house mice, cockroaches and myriads of other insects. Fungi and moulds grow, and even larger plants. This is an almost unexplored world as no one encourages this type of life! Rats, mice, cockroaches and other vermin are ruthlessly destroyed. Yet they are the most successful creatures in London for, after centuries of determined effort, man still cannot rid himself of them.

Some of the vermin are becoming rare. The black rat once widespread over much of Britain now has London, mainly around the docks, as one of its few strongholds, though it is also found in the Oxford Street area. A declining species, it is unlikely to get legal protection should it be in danger of extinction.

The house mice of London may be found everywhere, even in refrigerated meat stores. Dr Harrison-Matthews in *British Mammals* describes their occurrence as follows:

> The most unexpected environment in which house mice flourish is that provided by the cold stores in which meat is kept for long periods. In total darkness, and in a temperature never above 15° F (about −10° C) with no food other than meat, the mice breed and live their whole lives . . . They flourish . . . to an unusual extent so that the average size and weight of cold-store mice is above that of outside mice. Further their reproductive rate is higher; they produce an average of over 6½ litters per year compared with 5½ of domestic mice; the average number of young in each litter is also greater being over 6⅓ against a fraction above 5½.

In the older and scruffier parts of London even the human inhabitants may carry an interesting fauna, though my entomologist friends assure me that fleas and lice are becoming quite rare.

From Whitehall, Buckingham Palace, Downing Street, Westminster Abbey and several other buildings in central London the unusual spider *Segestria florentina* has been recorded. This species grows up to an inch or so in length and has shiny metallic-green chelicerae. It lives in a silk tube which is built in a crack in a wall or in bark. From the rim of the tube a number of threads extend; if these are tapped gently the inhabitant rushes out and attacks violently. *S. florentina* is mainly found in cities in southern England and it seems likely that it is an introduced species. W. S. Bristowe in *The World of Spiders* describes how he recorded three species previously unknown in Britain and subsequently found them living quite unnoticed in the British Museum (Natural History) in South Kensington. They were *Oonops domesticus*, *Physocyclus simoni* and *Euophrys lanigera*; the latter, a jumping spider, is usually recorded from the roofs of buildings and has been found on the roof of the Oxford Natural History Museum as well as the South Kensington Museum.

SOME RARITIES

Although Kew Gardens are well outside the confines of central London, it is perhaps worth mentioning that several exotic species of insects and spiders have been recorded in the hothouses there from time to time, as well as the occasional reptile and amphibian. Only rarely do they manage to establish themselves, but in 1969 a thriving colony of the tropical spider *Coleosoma floridanum* was discovered in one of the hot-houses.

From time to time whales and seals are seen in the River Thames. Over the last decade some three or four common seals have been spotted, both below the city and as far up the river as Richmond. The whales seen in the Thames include a lesser rorqual and a bottle-nosed dolphin which was stranded in East India Dock. The chances of being able to see seals and porpoises in the Thames are remote, but somehow it is difficult to resist a look every time one walks over the Thames!

For the ornithologist wandering around in the city the best advice is to keep a sharp lookout, wherever he is, particularly

Page 35 (*above*) Small elephant hawk moth, a species which is not uncommon in London, occurring on rosebay willow herb; (*below*) woodlice (*Oniscus asellus*) are one of the many invertebrates which can be found throughout the city, even right in the centre

Page 36 (*above*) An albino blackbird in Hyde Park. Albinism seems fairly widespread among London's birds—it has been suggested that in towns natural selection against such birds is not as great as in rural areas; (*below*) the black redstart could probably be regarded as London's bird. The story of their colonisation of the city bombed sites is an interesting example of a bird adapting to man-made environment

in spring or autumn. A water rail was once seen on the window-sill of the Guildhall and a corncrake has been noted by St Thomas's Hospital. Along the foreshore of the Thames in central London, common sandpipers have often been seen as well as redshank and oystercatcher.

The occasional rare butterfly or moth turns up even in the heart of London; as recently as 1967 the rare and beautiful Camberwell beauty was seen resting for a few brief moments on the bumper of a parked car in Kensington. Incidentally, painted lady and red admiral butterflies, and the humming bird hawk moth, are all migrant species which often occur well into the built-up area.

London is a place where very often the unexpected is all that can be expected and for that reason a naturalist should examine with care every bird seen, every young plant trying to gain a foothold on a window sill. Even if they are common species they need recording and documenting—the environment is changing so rapidly that they may become rare within a decade.

CHAPTER THREE

The suburban sprawl

General picture—Particular sites

GENERAL PICTURE

LONDON SPRAWLS OUT over a vast area and most of the human inhabitants dwell in the suburbs which straggle across the countryside which once surrounded the city of London. Yet these suburbs provide an interesting habitat for a variety of wildlife.

Whereas the centre of London tends to be arid and bare of vegetation, the suburbs show a tendency to an almost excessive richness. Plants are carefully watered, regularly fertilised, neatly pruned and trimmed and generally fussed over by thousands of amateur gardeners. An aerial photograph of the London suburbs shows the considerable extent to which gardens dominate the landscape. Beautiful herbaceous borders, roses, lawns as smooth as billiard tables, enormous marrows and so on are the net results of the suburban gardeners' toil and sweat, but many gardens are unkempt and it is from these 'hippies' among the respectable rows of 'semi-detacheds' that many of the weeds and insect pests originate. The gardener then spends many hours trying to eradicate the rich fauna of insect pests which his rich flora of exotic plants has undoubtedly attracted.

Mammals

The abundant supply of insects has attracted a number of animals, in particular the hedgehog. Hedgehogs have been encouraged to such an extent that there is probably a higher density of them living in suburbia than in any other habitat. They are even found in industrial buildings; Bromley gasworks in east London is a noted haunt, for instance. They are only rarely seen wandering around during daytime, being mainly nocturnal animals, and most of the data on their occurrence and distribution has been gained from records of their flattened remains on roads. The hedgehog's main defence against any aggressor is to roll itself up into a ball and present an impenetrable mass of spines; this behaviour works very well for cats and dogs and most other intruders, but not for any motor vehicles it may encounter during its nocturnal wanderings. It is for this reason that the squashed remains of hedgehogs are a common sight around London. Very recent observations suggest that in some suburban areas it is becoming quite common for hedgehogs not to roll up at the approach of such danger, but to run off. A change in behaviour such as this will undoubtedly have great survival value in a population of hedgehogs whose greatest single enemy is probably the motor car.

Many people encourage hedgehogs to visit their gardens by placing bowls of milk on the lawn, usually near a compost heap or other attractive spot. Once the hedgehog has started visiting the spot regularly, the bowl may gradually be moved nearer the house until the occupants have the pleasure of observing their local hedgehogs every evening in the light shed from the windows.

Hedgehogs hibernate, but observations made in London show that they can be active in all months of the year, though the number of individuals observed in January, February and March is only between 5 per cent and 10 per cent of the number recorded in August. At some time during the summer the hedgehogs may quite readily bring their family, usually about five in number, along to the feeding bowl. Gardeners sometimes find nests of young hedgehogs, soft-spined pink-nosed and helpless, hidden away in the unkempt parts of the garden. In London, nests containing young have been found in every month from April until October, with the exception of June; but only single nests have been observed in April, May and October, indicating that the peak breeding season is July to August.

In the suburbs the habit of feeding wild animals has sometimes spread to even larger species of mammals, although few people would believe that in the suburbs both foxes and badgers exist. A few years ago members of the London Natural History Society investigated the status of these two animals—an enquiry known to the participants as the 'Brock and Tod' survey. From this preliminary investigation and the subsequent accumulation of observations, together with past records, the organiser, W. G. Teagle, was able to draw a detailed picture of the status of badgers and foxes in and around London.

The supporters of the ancient and barbaric practice of hunting foxes with dogs often used to argue that they helped to conserve the fox; if they stopped hunting, farmers, game preservers, etc, would soon exterminate foxes altogether. This is an argument which is easily discredited in many places, not least in the London suburbs where it is almost as impossible to get rid of foxes as it is for the hunt to follow them. Although foxes have been expanding into the outer suburbs for some considerable time it is only in the last decade or so that naturalists have made any serious efforts to study them in this environment. It has now been found that they extend well into London, often occurring well into the more urbanised central areas. One was discovered in Hyde Park, though this individual could well have been a released or escaped pet. It is likely, however, that most of the foxes, even near the centre, are wild ones which have wandered.

The best places to see foxes are along the railway embankments, particularly on the suburban routes in Kent. The cubs seen by commuters travelling to London will ultimately disperse, and by what more logical way than along the railway lines whose embankments form green arteries pushing well into the heart of London. The breeding site closest to the centre was, however, not particularly close to any railway line, except the Underground. This was the earth of a pair of foxes which in 1958, closely watched by local residents, reared a family on some

waste ground opposite Stockwell tube station. It is probable
that almost any suitable area in the London suburbs—large
gardens, waste ground, parks, etc—will be colonised by foxes.
Not only do the latter stray considerable distances when the
young disperse, but the individual territory of each fox is large
and, as it will often cross roads which run through its territory,
there is a reasonable chance of catching a brief glimpse of one
suddenly illuminated in the headlamps of a car driven through
the suburbs late at night.

The keen fox-watcher who wants to track down an earth
will have no difficulty in London. Each spring one or more pairs
of suburban foxes usually manage to get their picture in a local
newspaper, sometimes even the national press, and after a few
enquiries it is not difficult to trace the earth. The author's first
encounter with his local fox in Wimbledon is typical of the way
most people become aware of such a presence in the neighbourhood. One evening his dustbin lid fell to the ground with a
crash, at the end of the garden. There was no wind so he decided
to investigate and, on his approach, a fox leapt nimbly on to the
coal-shed roof and then on to a high wall. It paused briefly,
silhouetted against the sky and then disappeared, leaving the
characteristic strong musky scent behind it. Once smelt this
odour is usually recognised without difficulty and can sometimes
be detected even when a fox has merely crossed an area. For a
fox, the transition from raiding a dustbin to coming for bones
put out for it on the lawn is an easy one, and with patience foxes
can be encouraged to feed in the light falling from the windows
of the house in the manner described for hedgehogs.

In some parts of the outer suburbs the habit of encouraging
wild mammals to visit gardens has extended to badgers, usually
considered to be very shy and wary of humans. Normally nocturnal, badgers can easily pass unnoticed, in fact in some places
they can be extremely difficult to see, so sensitive are they to
man's activity after centuries of senseless persecution. But in
London's suburbs badgers are usually encouraged rather than
persecuted. In the survey of badgers in and around London the

large gardens and grounds of hospitals, colleges and similar institutional buildings were often found to have setts in them. The occupiers of the property are usually proud of their badgers and tolerate any damage the badgers may do to fences or the odd plant.

Another mammal well established in the suburbs is the grey squirrel. Originally a North American species, the animals found in Britain are the descendants of captives released around the turn of the century. The grey squirrel colonised most of Britain very rapidly and for many years was held responsible for the decline of the native red squirrel, which decreased and disappeared from many parts of its range at about the same time as the grey squirrel made its appearance. It is now thought that the decline of the red squirrel was independent of the increase of the American species.

The grey squirrel became a pest in many woodland areas and the Ministry of Agriculture, Fisheries & Food undertook various measures, most of which were unsuccessful, to exterminate or at least control them. The grey squirrel is firmly established, but one legacy of the attempts in the past to control them is that large numbers of people still regard them as vermin. Whilst this may be true in rural areas and in forestry plantations, it is probably not true in suburban areas. They may do occasional damage to trees but this is small harm compared with their amenity value of giving people the pleasure of seeing such active and playful animals in the wild. Though 'wild', grey squirrels are often remarkably tame and confiding, and in recent years Londoners have become more tolerant towards them, often feeding them and making them tame enough to feed from the hand. Many of London's parks and recreation grounds have one or more resident squirrels which will come scampering down from the tree tops for a handful of peanuts or similar delicacy.

In the outer suburbs around Banstead, Whyteleafe and Coulsdon in Surrey, there are a number of albino and partial albino grey squirrels. In some species of animal albinism is not uncommon, but it is relatively rare in grey squirrels.

The wood mouse *Apodemus sylvaticus*, or long-tailed field mouse as it is sometimes known, is a typically suburban mammal at least in the outer suburbs of London. There it often replaces the house mouse as a domestic pest, though it does not normally reach the latter's population density. The wood mouse is a domestic nuisance rather than a pest, a few individuals moving into the warmth of an outhouse or kitchen during the winter months, but generally moving out again in the summer. Wood mice are easily distinguished from house mice. The wood mouse is a warm russet colour with large ears, large eyes and jumps erratically in leaps and bounds when disturbed. The house mouse is 'mouse' coloured with less noticeable ears and eyes and runs almost as if it is being propelled on wheels.

Closely related to the wood mouse is the yellow-necked mouse *A. flavicollis*. This species, though superficially similar, is larger and more strikingly marked. Its distribution throughout England and Wales is patchy and discontinuous, as it is around London. It is only regularly recorded from outer suburban areas in south Essex, north-west Surrey and some parts of Kent.

A mammal which has not yet succeeded in becoming established in London or elsewhere, but may well do so in the future, is the golden hamster *Mesocricetus auratus*. This popular pet is far from popular with officials of the Ministry of Agriculture, Fisheries & Food who see it as a potentially dangerous pest. Small colonies have established themselves, usually as a result of escapes from pet shops, in several parts of England as far apart as Suffolk and Lancashire. The largest colony recorded so far was found at Bury St Edmunds. When the authorities were called to investigate, over 230 animals were trapped or killed. Like rats and mice, golden hamsters have a high reproductive potential, but unlike the former, hamsters can survive inclement weather by hibernating. They are also great hoarders of food and make extensive tunnels, both factors making them difficult to deal with should they ever reach pest proportions.

It is mainly in small towns or suburban areas that hamsters have escaped and established themselves, not surprisingly as this is where most pet shops are situated. The colonies are usually close to such a shop as these are usually the only places with two or more hamsters—as a pet animal they are always kept singly. The only major outbreak of hamsters in the London suburbs recorded so far was in 1960. In August of that year four individuals were believed to have escaped from a pet shop in Finchley, Middlesex, and about six months later extensive tunnels and hoards of food were found beneath the premises. During the next nine months more than twenty hamsters were either trapped alive or poisoned. During the winter months of November to March no more were seen, as they were probably hibernating, but in the following spring another three were found. Interesting as golden hamsters may be to any naturalist finding a colony of them living in the wild, they should always be reported to the authorities as soon as possible.

Though it can hardly be considered a 'wild' animal, the cat plays a very important part in the suburban ecosystem. In most parts of the suburbs predators on birds are extinct or rare. Small boys may be significant egg-predators in some areas and cars also take a significant toll, but cats are probably one of the most important preying species. Unfortunately, there is relatively little known about cats, it is mostly guesswork. Richard Fitter, author of *London's Natural History*, estimated London's cat population at 550,000 in 1949. Eric Simms, between 1951 and 1961 surveyed an area of suburbia in north London. He found that in an area of approximately 550 acres there were about 700 cats in 1951 and by 1961 the population had dropped to about 300, but no change in the bird population was noted. This is accounted for by the fact that the population of most species of birds, in suburban London, is limited by the availability of nest sites rather than predation.

Birds

Birds are apparent almost everywhere in the suburbs. Bread is put out for them at the very least, and many people go to con-

siderable trouble in constructing elaborate bird tables to accom-
modate the avian banquets they supply daily. The suburban
vegetation is rich, but most of it dies down during the winter,
and whereas normally birds suffer from food shortages when the
seeds and berries have gone and there are no insects available,
the suburbs are littered with crusts, bacon rind, canary seed and
a variety of other foods put out especially for them. The result
is that there is a very rich bird fauna.

Tits are some of the most popular garden birds, and probably
the group which benefits most of all from the food put out.
During a severe winter they normally die off in large numbers,
unable to find sufficient food during the short hours of daylight
in order to survive the long cold night. In the suburbs the fat
and bacon rinds, rich in energy, supply the crucial survival
rations. Undoubtedly the commonest tits are the blue tit and
great tit. The small blue tit is always popular, being an acrobat
of considerable talent. A string of peanuts, threaded whilst still
in the 'shell', will provide hours of entertainment as he extracts
each nut. An interesting habit which appears and then disappears
only to reappear a few years later, is their pecking through the
caps of milk bottles in order to obtain the cream at the top of the
milk. Both great tit and blue tit partake, but in south London it
is more often great tits. Presumably the habit was acquired first
of all by an inquisitive tit finding a slightly leaky milk bottle
or one that had been left out in severe frost, the milk having
expanded on freezing and pushed the top off. Having found that
the top end of a milk bottle contains something very tasty, the
tits soon learnt to extract it themselves.

Coal tits are also abundant in the suburbs, the marsh tit less
so, and the willow tit is only a rare visitor. The tits all respond not
only to artificial feeding grounds but also to artificial nest sites.
Many suburban gardens contain nest boxes, and without these
it is doubtful whether there would be anything like the present
tit population. Suburban gardens usually lack old trees, and old
trees with holes are normally necessary for nesting—a nest box
in a garden is a sure way of attracting them.

Just as suburban tits have adapted to milk bottles and garden boxes to nest in, so the great spotted woodpecker has found a new source of food in the nest boxes. Occasionally boxes containing nesting tits have had the hole enlarged and the young eaten by this beautiful bird. The solution to this problem is straightforward, the area around the hole of the nest box is protected by a metal plate. Great spotted woodpeckers are normally fairly shy, but in recent years have been visiting gardens more and more frequently, a trend likely to continue as they, like the tits, often suffer severe reductions in numbers in hard winters but find ample food on bird tables. The great spotted woodpecker is the most frequent of woodpecker visitors, and can be attracted by cob nuts or by large pieces of fat tied to the branch of a tree. The green woodpecker is a less frequent visitor to gardens, but in areas where are large parks nearby will often visit gardens in search of ants, one of its favourite foods. The lesser spotted woodpecker is often overlooked, being smaller and generally more secretive than the other two species, but as yet it does not seem to have really colonised the suburbs.

Superficially similar in habits to the woodpeckers, the nuthatch is an increasingly frequent visitor to the bird table, particularly during the winter months. As yet it has not really adapted to nest boxes, possibly they are not placed high enough in the trees, and consequently it seems that the availability of nest sites is one of the factors limiting its spread into the suburbs. The nest of a nuthatch is unique among British birds. In order to ensure the hole in which they are going to nest is small enough to exclude unwelcome intruders, the birds plaster the perimeter of the hole with mud. On many occasions whilst observing nuthatches at work in suburban parks and gardens the author has seen the bold and aggressive starlings take over the hole, but they can only do this when the work of plastering has just commenced; later the hole will be too small for a starling to get into.

Blackbirds, song thrushes, robins and dunnocks nest throughout suburban London, wherever there are large enough gardens, and their breeding density is often exceptionally high. Other species also nest more or less throughout the suburbs, depending on the availability of nest sites. Robins have long been famous for choosing strange nesting places—old kettles, the pocket of a coat hanging in an outhouse and so forth. On the continent this bird is normally shy and rarely approaches man, but in Britain, as every gardener knows, the robin is confident, almost cheeky, as it waits for the earth to be turned and snatches a worm. Blackbirds often choose equally bizarre nest sites—gas meters, cars, lamp posts and many other strange places have been recorded. Blue tits, also finding a shortage of natural nest sites, have even nested inside a London Transport bus stop.

The naturalist Eric Simms made a detailed study of the bird life of Dollis Hill in Middlesex over a period of ten years. The area he examined is typical suburbia and here he found the density of birds to be approximately 52 to 53 birds per 10 acres. This is much higher than the 19 to 22 birds per 10 acres recorded in Regent's Park, but lower than the 98 per 10 acres recorded in the late 1930s for Kensington. The national average density for built-up areas is about 50 birds per 10 acres (the same as for mixed woodland) and so it would appear that Dollis Hill is fairly typical. Over 20 species of birds bred regularly though many only in small numbers.

The mistle thrush, chaffinch, greenfinch, bullfinch and wren are all widespread, breeding throughout the suburbs. There is an even longer list of birds which breed in small numbers, scattered throughout the suburban area, restricted either by lack of suitable nesting sites or lack of suitable feeding areas. Some of these species are in the process of adapting to the environment and their populations increase steadily year by year: kestrels, tawny owls, blackcaps, spotted flycatchers, pied wagtails, linnets, goldfinches, house martins, swifts and several other species. Although the availability of food must play some part in their population control, particularly in an unnatural environment such as London, it seems more likely that the availability of nest sites is the main factor involved. One of the reasons that tits, robins, blackbirds and kestrels have large suburban populations is that they have adapted to an environment modified by man and taken advantage of the nest sites it provides. It is rather unaccountable then that the swifts and house martins—two species which have long been closely associated with man, building their nests in or on his houses—should have such stable and relatively confined breeding populations in the London suburbs. In recent years only slight increases have been observed in the number of house martins and only a few new areas have been colonised, so that overall they are much more restricted than other 'suburban' birds and not actively expanding and colonising. The reasons for this are obscure and have provided much food for thought for more than one suburban naturalist. It may well be that the swift is to some degree limited by the availability of food but mainly by the availability of nest sites as it tends to prefer older style buildings which are, of course, declining; the house martin could be limited by the availability of suitable mud with which to build its nest.

An interesting example of an expanding species is the collared dove. Originally found in east Europe and Asia Minor this species started spreading through Europe in the 1930s. It first occurred in Britain in the 1950s and from one pair in 1955 the breeding population in Britain rose to somewhere in the region of 20,000 pairs by the mid 1960s. The collared dove has only recently penetrated the suburbs of London, though it has been well established on the fringes of the city for some years, particularly in areas with allotments and smallholdings. It was not until April 1971 that the author saw his first central-London collared dove—on a roof top in the Strand. One wonders why the collared dove has not colonised the central parks of London and the inner suburbs as they are extremely abundant in similar situations in Holland, Yugoslavia, Romania and even Birmingham. The only explanation seems to be that in London other birds, particularly the feral pigeon and wood pigeon, are well established and in the face of this competition the collared dove has not yet managed to gain a foothold. The wood pigeon is not normally an urban bird and it is just possible that the very fact of the presence of this species is preventing the collared dove from colonising London. These are the type of problems to which any naturalist, with patience, could possibly supply the answer, provided accurate data were first collected.

Not all suburbia is gardens and allotments. Scattered throughout it are many factories and other industrial sites. These may not appear to be an ideal habitat for wildlife and, in fact, they are not ideal—but some wildlife does manage to find a foothold. The power stations, gasworks, large railway depots and so on all have a few features in common; features which are also shared with the bombed sites. They are large, often have a high level of atmospheric pollution, and usually have a fairly low level of human disturbance. The absence of disturbance is likely to encourage birds to nest.

Which birds are likely to nest in the industrial sites? One of the most obvious, since it can often be seen at and around the cooling towers of power stations, is the kestrel. The few ledges, remote and inaccessible, available on these sites are ideal for such a bird. Pied wagtails are another bird to which concrete bricks are as good as natural cliffs. But the black redstart, a bird which created ornithological headlines during World War II by nesting in the central London bombed sites (see page 50), has now colonised the industrial sites of the suburbs. Just as London is the capital for the human population of Britain so it is for the black redstart.

It was in the early 1960s that these birds were noted breeding regularly away from the city on industrialised sites—a few pairs were known to nest around power stations. This move was hardly surprising as the very first black redstarts to breed in London were the three pairs which occupied the Wembley Palace of Engineering the year after the Wembley exhibition closed in 1926. Between this date and the colonisation of the bombed sites in 1942 odd pairs bred in a shed at Woolwich Arsenal, in the precincts of Westminster Abbey and in a bombed site in Wandsworth.

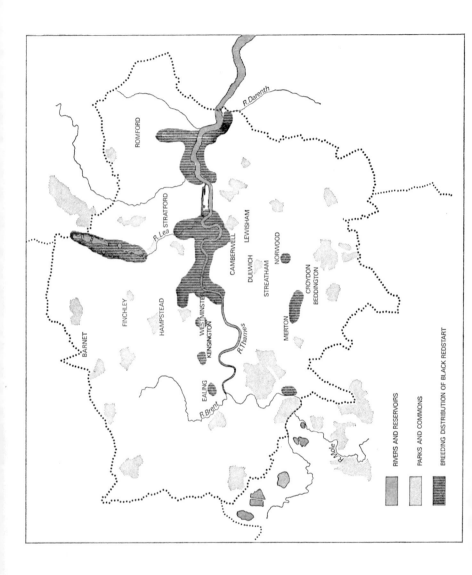

RIVERS AND RESERVOIRS

PARKS AND COMMONS

BREEDING DISTRIBUTION OF BLACK REDSTART

ROMFORD

R.Darenth

STRATFORD

R.Lea

CAMBERWELL

LEWISHAM

DULWICH

STREATHAM

NORWOOD

CROYDON

BEDDINGTON

FINCHLEY

HAMPSTEAD

WESTMINSTER

KENSINGTON

MERTON

BARNET

R.Thames

EALING

R.Brent

R.Mole

In 1964 Brian Meadows made a survey of the heavily industrialised areas of the lower reaches of the River Lea. Here he discovered at least four pairs. Since then other breeding localities have been discovered nearby, all in areas of concentrated industry, around power stations, gasworks, railway sidings, etc. Although it is possible that the population formerly breeding in central London has moved outwards to such sites, it is probable that black redstarts have been breeding on industrial sites for some time and that their nesting anywhere other than the bombed sites has been overlooked; after all very few birdwatchers would think of visiting a power station to look for one of Britain's rarest breeding birds. But this is in fact the sort of habitat in which to look for them, and hardly a year goes by without a new breeding locality being discovered. They are difficult birds to locate—the singing male may be completely overwhelmed by the sound of railways or machinery and a small blackish bird with a rufous tail may be distinctive when you do see it, but very difficult to locate in an acre of towers, walls, sheds and so forth.

In recent years black redstarts have been recorded as breeding, or attempting to breed, at the following places: the pumping station for King George V reservoir in Essex; Littlebrook and Elmers End in Kent; Croydon power station near Beddington; Croydon in Surrey; Tottenham gasworks; White City; Brimsdown power station and Shepherds Bush in Middlesex. It will be interesting to see if it establishes itself as an urban bird in the same way that house martins, swifts and house sparrows have done. Russian ornithologists have noticed this change in habitat and it seems very likely that one of the reasons for the expansion of the black redstart's range in the last half century or so is that it has managed to adapt to a life in the manmade environment of villages and cities. Perhaps in a few decades the song of a black redstart will become a familiar sound—the nightingale's song of the town.

Flora

The gardens of suburbia are responsible for some of the most interesting species of London's flora. Michaelmas daisies *Aster novae-belgiae* will spring up on waste ground and untended gardens; Japanese polygonum *Polygonum cuspidatum*, golden rod *Solidago virgaurea* and buddlia *Buddlia davidii* from China are other well-established garden escapes. Such escapes are of considerable interest to botanists because the relative abundance of the more widespread species is always changing as new species gain a foothold. Amongst the more spectacular examples are the giant hogweed *Heracleum mantigazzeanum*—it grows up to ten feet tall and its spread received a lot of publicity in the national press—and the Himalayan balsam *Impatiens glandulifera* which has very explosive fruit and is particularly widespread in north London.

Besides being colonised by garden escapes, waste ground in the suburbs particularly is invaded by the seeds of wild flowers. Each year buildings are levelled and new ones replace them, but sometimes the site may be vacant for a year or more. When this happens, plants soon grow. The vacant site destined to become the new Covent Garden market is, at the time of writing, well overgrown with willowherbs and a variety of other plants. Mugwort *Artemesia vulgaris*, creeping thistle *Cirsium arvense*, coltsfoot *Tussilago farfara*, cocksfoot *Dactylis glomerata*, are all common wild flowers which soon become established. Bindweeds, *Calystegia* spp, climb over fences and, to complete a picture of the commoner plants, mention must be made of the grasses—meadow grass *Poa annua*, oat grass *Arrhenatherum elatior*, brooms *Bromus* spp and knot grass *Polygonum aviculare* are all common and widespread.

The pavements which line the suburban streets are another manmade habitat well worth studying. As far as the author knows no detailed study of them has been undertaken, and yet even a superficial glance indicates that flowering cherries, so (*right*) Starlings—the commuters in reverse. As Londoner's forsake Trafalgar and Parliament Squares, the starlings are arriving in the evening to roost

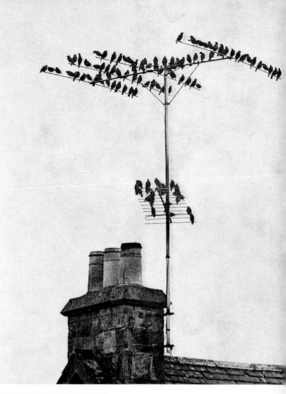

(*left*) kestrels are surprisingly widespread in London, this one was photographed at her nest in one of the BBC buildings near Oxford Circus

Page 54 (*above*) Generally ignored by naturalists, but very much a part of London's wildlife—the London pigeon. It is a feral decendant of the domesticated rock dove; (*below*) the London plane is of hybrid origins. It survives well in the grime of London because it sheds its dirt-laden bark regularly

popular in North Croydon, are replaced by mutilated lime trees in parts of Streatham. The pollarding which most of the borough councils practise tends to be crude and reduces the trees to sprouting stumps, but birds can nest in them and insects flourish. The lime trees, particularly those in the south-eastern suburbs, are still a good place to look for lime hawk moths and their larvae.

In his paper on suburban bird-life Eric Simms described the trees he encountered in Dollis Hill, Middlesex, a typical London suburb. They were elms, mountain ash, London plane, horse chestnut, tree-of-heaven, sycamore, acacia, Norway maple, silver maple, silver birch, several species of *Crategus* and *Prunus*, laburnum, poplar, white-beam, crab-apple, white willow, lime and ash. Many of these species, planted when the estate was laid out, are unsuitable for suburban streets and gardens and will doubtless be gradually removed as they reach maturity.

To sum up the history of suburban natural history, it is important that *all* living things should be considered including cats, dogs, London pigeons and humans. Their population density considerably affects the suburban wildlife, but most naturalists ignore such aspects.

PARTICULAR SITES

Around Norwood

One particularly interesting area occurs in south London centred on Norwood, whose name is derived from 'north wood'—and several portions of the Great North Wood still remain. The largest is known as Dulwich Woods, permission to visit which must be obtained from the Estates Governors of Dulwich College. The dominant trees in the woods are sessile oak *Quercus petraea*. These are straight-trunked, tall and form a dense canopy. The undergrowth is largely free from trampling and has a rich flora, undoubtedly the richest woodland flora within six miles of St Paul's Cathedral.

D

As one would expect, the fauna is also rich; a few years ago even the crested newt was recorded, though whether or not any survive now is doubtful. Foxes, hedgehogs, bank voles, grey squirrels and wood mice are all abundant. The birds are interesting and the top of the adjacent golf course is an excellent spot for migration watching. The breeding birds include such species as tree creeper, all three woodpeckers, cuckoo, marsh tit, long-tailed tit, whitethroat, garden warbler, blackcap, chiffchaff and willow warbler. Redpolls, siskins and tits gather in winter and many other species of birds are recorded each year.

Elsewhere in south London smaller relics of the Great North Wood occur. By no means as well preserved as the privately owned Dulwich Woods, they often have a good show of blue-bells in spring and a surprising number of plants and birds survive the trampling and plundering of small boys. Grange-wood (TQ 3268) near Thornton Heath is the most heavily trampled relic and little of the original ground flora survives. Holly, often associated with sessile oak, is plentiful and in spring there is a good show of bluebells. Biggin Wood, Norbury (TQ 3170) is less trampled and has an area which contains many introduced exotics such as laurels and rhododendrons. The bird life is fairly rich: blackcap, nuthatch, great spotted woodpecker, green woodpecker, marsh and coal tits all breed. Slow worms still occur and a few common frogs, common toads, smooth newts and crested newts breed in garden ponds adjacent to the wood.

Abbey Wood, Charlton Pit and the Kent marshes

Bluebells and daffodils are characteristic of mixed woodland in spring, and Abbey Wood (TQ 4878) on the eastern edge of the suburbs is no exception. Abbey Wood is classified as a Site of Special Scientific Interest (sssi) by the Nature Conservancy, and a permit must be obtained before visiting from the Chief Parks Officer, GLC Parks Department, Cavell House, 2A Charing Cross, London, WC2. The interest of Abbey Wood is not so much the plant and animal life, though it is well worth observing, but the highly fossiliferous Lower Eocene Blackheath Beds. They were originally discovered when William Whitaker, working for the Geological Survey, noticed sharks' teeth and molluscs outside rabbit burrows.

Casual visitors are not allowed to excavate the important seams, some six feet below the surface, but are allowed to sift the spoil heaps. The sands are mainly fine, intermingled with black flint pebbles. Mammal remains are rare, but reptiles such as crocodiles and turtles are slightly commoner. The shell seams also contain many sharks' teeth. The commonest are those of *Odontaspis* and the most abundant molluscs are the marine *Corbicula*, *Glycymeris melanopsis* and *Brotia*. Some shells such as *Theodoxus* may even show the original colouration.

Even closer in towards London is Charlton Pit (TQ 4178). Sometimes known as Gilbert's Pit, it was originally quarried to obtain sand for moulding purposes at the Royal Arsenal in Woolwich. It also is an sssi and a permit must be obtained from the GLC Parks Department before visiting.

Some parts of the cliff are fifty feet high and visitors should be careful not to start a landslide. One of the most interesting features of the pit is that it shows a fine sequence of the Woolwich Beds. The succession visible is Thanet Sands, Woolwich Bottom Bed, Woolwich Beds (with shells and Lewisham Leaf Bed) and the Blackheath Beds. The Woolwich Beds show a rhythm of sedimentation which is a 'text-book classic'—the base is a pebble-bed about one foot thick, consisting of black rounded flint pebbles; the next beds are glanconitic marine sands, which are below the esturine shell beds. Above the shell beds are the lagoonal silts with the imprints of leaves (Lewisham Leaf Beds). The shell beds stand out clearly as striped clays, and the most abundant fossils are *Corbicula*, *Brotia* and *Tympanotonus*. Oysters occur in a band at the base of the shell bed. Many of the fossils are very fragile and suitable collecting boxes and equipment should be taken when visiting. The chalk (Coranguinum Zone) is exposed nearby in a section behind a block of flats opposite Charlton football ground, in Grove Valley.

The few remaining marshes nearby have relics of the seaside flora which is well worth examining, and a few years ago the great green grasshopper occurred on Abbey Wood and Belvedere Marshes and also at Dartford and Plumstead. In recent years spectacular numbers of waders and waterfowl have been recorded on and beside the Thames in this area, and each year the numbers of birds seen grows more and more impressive. The ornithologist Peter Grant recently published a brief report and notes in the *London Bird Report* to the effect that in 1970 maxima of over 1,500 shelduck, 700 mallard, 700 teal, over 300 pintail, 800 tufted duck and 2,500 pochard were recorded during January and February on the Thames between Woolwich and Cross Ness. Gadwall, wigeon, shoveler, scaup, goldeneye and smew were also recorded. The duck are by no means confined to this particular area; other flocks can be found in Rainham, Erith, Swanscombe and Stone.

The discovery of these wintering waterfowl on the Thames is a very recent event and has caused considerable excitement amongst ornithologists. Although the decrease in pollutants in the Thames may be a contributing factor, other more temporary causes, such as the weather conditions in Holland, have undoubtedly had an effect. It is believed that the draining of other wintering grounds such as in the Haringvtet area of Holland may also be involved but as yet this idea has not been researched. Future developments of the marshlands adjoining the Thames may well jeopardise the future of the wintering duck, as may the construction of the tidal barrage at Woolwich, designed to protect London from a flood disaster. On Rainham Marsh flocks of up to 140 brambling were recorded, and in autumn it is particularly productive for waders. Maxima of 20 little stints, 3 Temminck's stints, 50 dunlin, 35 little ringed plovers, 20 curlew sandpipers, 50 green sandpipers, 6 wood sandpipers, 50 common sandpipers and small numbers of spotted redshank, redshank, greenshank, curlew, black-tailed godwit, ruff, jack snipe and several other species were all recorded in 1970. This area is one of the most important sites in the London district and is almost entirely surrounded by the built-up area.

Other sites on the Thames

Further up the River Thames is another opportunity for finding fossils, this time on the Thames foreshore. Keen gardeners on their way to visit Syon House (TQ 1676) would do well to make a brief detour as the site is opposite Church Street, some 300 yards downstream from the pavilion in Syon Park. At low tide patches of London Clay (Lower Eocene) can be seen. Some of the larger fossils may be found on the spot, but the best method of collecting is to take home a bulk sample of clay and treat it as described on page 22. This will leave behind all the fossils except the foraminifera, ostracods and other microfossils. Molluscs are the commonest fossils, with some worm tubes *Ditrupa* and a few fish teeth and otoliths. Further downstream are seams of Holocene freshwater shells of a more modern fauna; these can be collected by the same method. The great advantage of geology as a natural history pursuit is that the sites are reasonably predictable; the island known as Chiswick Eyot, further downstream between Barnes and Hammersmith bridges, is accessible at low tide, and on the south side of the island there are Holocene shell beds, from which over twenty species of molluscs have been recorded. Mammal remains have also been found.

The present-day flora and fauna of the river is also interesting. Even as far downstream as Chiswick and Barnes bridges the Thames still has some stretches of natural embankments, and those between Barnes and Isleworth are particularly interesting. In places patches of *Phragmites* and *Vitisalix* still exist together with many interesting remnants of the extensive Thameside marshes—marshes in which spoonbills nested in the sixteenth century, somewhere near what is now the King's Road.

One of the few places in London where the two-lipped door snail *Laciniaria biplicata* occurs is along this stretch of the river;

it has been recorded between Mortlake and Barnes on the south bank and around Chiswick on the north bank. Outside the London area this species is restricted to a few localities in Hertfordshire and Cambridgeshire. It is usually secretive by day, hiding amongst roots, and coming out on to the trunks of willows and other riverside trees at night.

CHAPTER FOUR

The Royal Parks

St James's Park–Hyde Park and Kensington Gardens–Richmond Park

THROUGHOUT THE WORLD the metropolis of London is famous for its parks and open spaces; few other large cities can boast anything like the number of public commons, parks, heaths, gardens, squares and playing fields, etc. Among all this greenness, although an arbitrary grouping, the Royal Parks of London form a reasonable unit, having certain features in common with each other distinguishing them from many of the other open spaces in London. All the Royal Parks are to a greater or lesser extent controlled and artificial, that is to say that they contain a high proportion of animals and plants which have been deliberately transported, often with considerable success.

The Royal Parks are Regent's Park together with Primrose Hill, Hyde Park and Kensington Gardens, Greenwich Park, Green Park, St James's Park, Richmond Park, Kew Gardens, Bushey Park and Hampton Court. Although technically not a Royal Park, Holland Park is usually treated under the same heading as it shares many features. The careful management and control of the habitat in the parks in many cases goes back two or three hundred years. They are now controlled by the Ministry of Public Building & Works (Department of the Environment). I have selected two of the most central parks and Richmond, the largest and most 'wild', for more detailed discussion.

ST JAMES'S PARK

Situated within a stone's throw of Trafalgar Square and Whitehall, St James's Park is the most central of the Royal Parks. It is, however, loosely connected with Green Park, which in turn is connected with Hyde Park and Kensington Gardens. Ever widening roads and road junctions are each year making this less apparent.

Around 1536 the park was first enclosed as a royal pleasure ground and in 1660 part of the Tyburn flowing through the park was converted into an ornamental canal. Both the park and this lake underwent several changes in design until, in 1827, John Nash laid out the whole in approximately the form in which it exists today. The present lake of over ten acres is of a completely different design to the earlier ones and is no longer fed by the Tyburn. Although it is a highly artificial habitat, it is an ideal one for many forms of wildlife and is well stocked with ornamental waterfowl including pelicans and cormorants. But apart from the pinioned collection there are many other birds in St James's. Some of the waterfowl, such as pochard and tufted duck, breed in the park, while others merely visit the lake to feed. In winter large numbers of pochard and tufted duck gather to feed as well as other species, and at odd times herons call in to feed.

The St James's Park lake has from time to time presented serious problems when it has become stagnant. Being such an artificial habitat it is prone to becoming ecologically unbalanced, and periodically it is cleaned out. This means that there is very little established natural life in the lake; fish have sometimes died in thousands due to lack of oxygen. From time to time plants have been introduced, but the waterfowl usually eat them. Some of the fish thrive whilst others die out almost immediately. The control of the various species of algae and the accumulations of mud had always been a difficult problem, and the lake is still far from balanced. Little is known about the invertebrates of the lake; in the past a dragonfly and aquatic snails have been found but as yet no thorough examination of the lake's fauna has been made.

Amongst the waterfowl on the lake are some Canada geese.

These large and rather aggressive birds have established themselves in and around London, flying between the various parks with stretches of open water, notably St James's, Hyde Park and the grounds of Buckingham Palace. In the central London area there are probably nearly 200 of them.

In St James's the wood pigeon of London can be seen at its best. Characteristic of the squares and parks, the wood pigeon has adapted to life in the urban habitat to an extent that few country dwellers would believe possible. Normally an extremely shy and wary bird, in London it has completely changed its ways. Though plenty of them nest in areas where there is barely a square yard of open ground, parks such as St James's provide the ideal habitat. There they feed on the never ending supply of crusts with which visitors seem to fill their pockets. The London wood pigeons are as tame as collared doves are in many European cities; it will be interesting to observe whether the feral pigeons and wood pigeons can be joined by a third species.

The ubiquitous house sparrow provides entertainment for many visitors to St James's. A good place is the bridge over the lake where, by holding out a handful of seed or breadcrumbs a party of sparrows is soon attracted down, and in no time at all is squabbling over a tasty morsel. There are tame sparrows in several other London parks.

Two other inhabitants which are surprising colonists are the moorhen and coot. Normally these birds are shy and retiring, and W. H. Hudson writing in the 1890s expressed surprise that the moorhen had recently nested in London. Nowadays everyone takes them for granted as is the case with the coot but, in fact, the first coot to nest in St James's were reared from introduced birds in 1926. Since then the numbers have increased to such an extent that the birds often have to nest in the flower beds, such is the competition for nest sites. For the amateur photographer both moorhen and coot then provide a unique opportunity to get portraits of what are often secretive species.

The most surprising colonist of all is one of the most recent—the herring gull. This is yet another example of how birds are learning to adapt to the urban environment and also of how man is learning not only to tolerate wildlife, but to encourage it. Herring gulls and lesser black-backed gulls have also nested in Regent's Park, no doubt attracted by the captive gulls in the London Zoo. Black-headed gulls are so used to humans that, in winter, they will feed from the hands of visitors.

Other breeding species, in this most central of London's parks include blue tits, song thrushes, blackbirds, robins and dunnocks. Some years chaffinches, mistle thrushes and wrens also nest.

HYDE PARK AND KENSINGTON GARDENS

Together these two parks form a large open area of varied habitats and, as one would expect, they support a considerable variety of wildlife.

Some of the trees in Kensington Gardens have grown to a considerable size and are the nesting site for a colony of jackdaws. The nesting success has been low for many years now and the colony is certainly on the verge of extinction, but a few birds can still be seen strutting around the Round Pond as children fish for three-spined sticklebacks closely supervised by their nannies (also in danger of extinction). The pondweeds of the Round Pond are of interest as some of them have not been recorded elsewhere in London. They include *Potamogeton pusillus*, *P. crispus*, *P. pectinatus* and *Zannichellia palustris*.

The plant life in many parts of central London is fascinating but can be a botanist's nightmare. So many of the plants are introductions either deliberate or, in many cases, accidental. In Hyde Park even the opium poppy *Papaver somniferum*—a popular garden plant—has been found. Visitors to the park feeding the birds are presumably responsible for the introduction of flax *Linum usitatissum*, canary grass *Phalaris canariensis* and millet *Panicum miliaceum*. The widespread grasshopper *Chorthippus brunneus* may also be an accidental introduction coming in with fodder for horses.

Birds are much in evidence and the number of species breeding is large, as might be expected from the habitat which is more diverse than St James's. The number and variety of birds found in London parks often surprise visitors. In the bird sanctuary in Kensington Gardens crows, jays, mistle thrushes, spotted flycatchers, blackcaps and coal tits are amongst the breeding birds, whilst a wide variety of others are commonly seen at certain times of the year, such as greenfinch, pied wagtail, willow warbler, redwing, tawny owl, stock dove and kestrel. For many years black-headed gulls which winter in the central parks and on the Thames Embankment have been studied, but surely the most astounding findings are those of J. Widgery who specialises in reading through binoculars the numbers on the rings of black-headed gulls. In one year he recorded 27 ringed birds in Hyde Park and Kensington Gardens, 10 of which were ringed in Finland, 1 in Russia, 1 in Czechoslovakia, 1 in Poland, 4 in Holland, 1 in Belgium and 8 in Britain. One bird had two rings —1 Danish and 1 Dutch.

The Round Pond and Long Water in Kensington Gardens and the Serpentine in Hyde Park provide a suitable habitat for mallard, tufted duck, Canada goose, mute swan, moorhen, coot and the occasional pochard—some even breed. In the winter large flocks of duck often congregate and on one occasion over 600 tufted duck were recorded. Occasionally more unusual waterfowl are seen on the Serpentine; in November 1969, within the space of a week, Slavonian, little and great-crested grebe were reported. In 1970 early in the morning three avocets were observed on the edge of the Serpentine and in 1971 kingfishers were seen. During July and August herons often visited the Serpentine to feed, possibly these are birds breeding in Regent's Park.

In Hyde Park to the north of the Serpentine is a memorial to W. H. Hudson, the author-naturalist. It is the famous statue by Epstein of Rima, heroine of Hudson's novel *Green Mansions*.

In 1898 Hudson published *Birds in London* which is one of the widely used starting points for discussing the changes in status of birds in and around the city. He also wrote several other essays and books connected in some way with London. The trees and undergrowth around the Hudson memorial are a well-known haunt of birds, and rarities such as the firecrest have been seen in its vicinity. The statue of Peter Pan is next to the enclosure in Kensington Gardens in which blackcaps breed and in which many warblers and other small birds have been seen. Another famous naturalist is also remembered in the gardens, this time with an obelisk—John Hanning Speke.

In these pollution-conscious days, it is comforting to know that the overall level of atmospheric pollution in the large area formed by Hyde Park and Kensington Gardens is lower than elsewhere in central London. It has been shown that many species of lichens, one of the simpler forms of plant life, are easily killed by high levels of atmospheric pollution. Whereas in St James's and Green Park only one species of lichen has been found, in Kensington Gardens six have been recorded.

Mammals occasionally turn up; bats have been seen on several occasions around the bridge over the Serpentine, but as yet the species has not been named as it is normally necessary to handle bats and examine them very closely in order to identify them. At dusk hedgehogs are sometimes to be seen, and probably breed in Kensington Gardens. The rabbits which are occasionally seen are most likely descendants partly from the captive colony that at one time existed in Hyde Park, and partly from released pets.

RICHMOND PARK

Situated on the outskirts of London, although it is now more or less completely surrounded by the suburbs, Richmond Park is probably the most interesting of all the Royal Parks to a naturalist.

If one enters the park by the Sheen Gate, nearby is the 'shrew-ash'. This, according to folk traditions, 'is an ash whose twigs

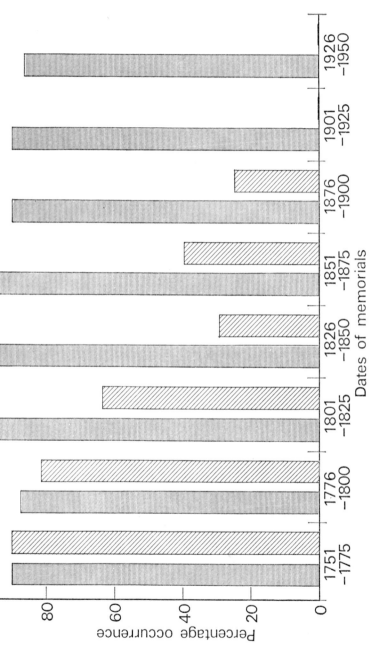

Histogram showing the percentage occurrence of two species of lichens on tombstones in St Peter and St Paul, Mitcham. By examining memorials, which are of course of known date, it was found that *Lecanora dispersa* (horizontal hatching) was able to colonise new surfaces whereas *Caloplaca heppiana* (diagonal hatching) was not found on any of the most recent memorials, and that as the pollution levels had risen, so the incidence of this species had fallen (after J. Laundon)

or branches, when gently applied to the limbs of cattle, will immediately relieve the pains which a beast suffers from the running of a shrew-mouse over the part affected'. When Gilbert White recorded this in 1776 regarding his parish of Selborne in Hampshire, the belief was already dying out, but he also noted how a shrew-ash was made. 'Into the body of the tree a deep hole was bored with an auger, and a poor devoted shrew-mouse was thrust in alive, and plugged in, no doubt, with several quaint incantations long since forgotten. As the ceremonies necessary for such a consecration are no longer understood, all succession is at an end and no such tree is known to subsist in the manor or hundred.' Dr Maurice Burton in 1957 wrote that there were people still living who could remember the Richmond shrew-ash being used as a cure for whooping cough. The tree itself is now in a rather decrepit state.

On arrival at Richmond some of the first animals to be seen are almost certain to be deer, for the park contains large herds of both red and fallow varieties. The best time to see them is October, during the rut, when the bellowing and the clashing of the antlers of the males can be heard all over the park. From the beginning of June onwards, the pretty dappled fawns are to be seen in the more secluded parts.

These are by no means the only mammals that can be found. Grey squirrels are common and around the Robin Hood Gate there is a small population which has an albinistic element in it, so that piebald squirrels are often seen. Throughout the park rabbits are common, though on a summer's day, with the hundreds of visitors that the park attracts, the chances of seeing rabbits are remote. Even more difficult to locate are the hares which still survive here. They often prefer to keep fairly near the cover of trees, particularly in winter when they can be described as essentially woodland animals. The small mammals are well represented: hedgehog, mole, common shrew, pygmy shrew, bank vole, field vole and wood mouse have all been recorded. Bats are commonly seen but positive identification is needed. The following species have been recorded within a few miles of the park and are quite likely to occur inside it: serotine, Leisler's, noctule, pipistrelle and long-eared. The badgers of Richmond Park are one of the colonies living closest to the centre of London. Only a few hundred yards from the Richmond Gate are Sidmouth Wood and Sawpit Plantation, peering in at dusk you may be lucky enough to catch a glimpse of one. Remarkably, it appears that stoats and weasels are absent and foxes rare. It may be that they have not been recorded, for the fox at any rate is common in the surrounding area.

Perhaps the most beautiful time to visit Richmond Park is in spring and you do not need to be a botanist or horticulturist to appreciate the Isabella Plantation. The rhododendrons and azalias, beneath a canopy of trees not yet in leaf or just opening are a riot of colour, and the paths through the plantation give an extremely pleasant walk. The Isabella Plantation is also an ideal spot for bird watching, particularly during the winter months. Near the top of the enclosure there is a large old tree stump on to which visitors regularly place food for the birds. If you observe from about ten feet away the following birds are almost certain to very soon appear: blue, great and coal tit, robin, and nuthatch. If you wait a little longer the following may also come: great-spotted woodpecker, long-tailed and marsh tit, greenfinch, bullfinch, chaffinch, redpoll, wren and goldcrest. Some of these will merely flit about in the nearby rhododendrons, attracted by the feeding birds. During the winter there is often a flock of redpolls. The plantations are also an ideal place for seeing the lesser spotted woodpecker, one of the most elusive of British birds. Shy and retiring, in springtime it is often bolder.

Richmond Park is one of the most popular recreational parks in London, but its large size means that a reasonable number of birds still manage to breed each year. A few redstarts, for instance, breed regularly in holes in the older trees, though before the war some twenty to twenty-five pairs bred annually. This decline in numbers is thought to be due to the fact that many of the suitable trees with nesting holes were cleaved. Also nesting in the older trees is a flourishing colony of jackdaws, surely one of the most attractive of British birds.

Other species of birds breeding in Richmond Park include blackcaps, whitethroats, willow warblers, chiffchaffs, garden warblers, spotted flycatchers and yellowhammers. In spring the plantations are a good place to get to grips with bird song. The birds are often used to human intruders, and can be approached fairly closely. Meadow pipits breed, as do tree pipits, the latter being one of the park's specialities. The list of breeding species is long, each year about fifty or more being recorded. This is about twice the number recorded breeding in Kensington Gardens and Hyde Park, and three times the number breeding in St James's Park.

Kestrels are nearly always visible in some part of the sky. In 1967 W. R. Ingram and B. A. Marsh studied theRichmond Park kestrels and found 20 pairs with territories—roughly 1 pair for each 125 acres of the 2,500 acres of the park. In that year it was believed that at least 54 young birds reached the flying stage. From these figures it is fairly obvious that Richmond Park is producing a considerable population surplus which pre-sumably accounts for some of the birds which are attempting to colonise the suburbs. The only other birds of prey which breed in the park are three species of owl. One pair of barn owls usually breed, and half a dozen or more each of tawny and little owls.

Of the many ponds in the park, the Pen Ponds are the only really large ones, and on them great-crested grebes and tufted duck breed most years. In the dense vegetation at the southern end of the Upper Pen Pond a few pairs of reed warblers breed, and water rails are sometimes seen.

Much of the low-lying land in Richmond Park is marshy during the winter months attracting reed buntings, and around the edges of these areas and in the woods, hares can sometimes be seen. In the marshes snipe and lapwing are frequent visitors and occasionally jack snipe and other more unusual species of wader have been seen. One of the most difficult waders to locate

Page 71
Every cellar,
loft, damp
unswept corner
is a potential
micro-nature
reserve, though
the animals are
rarely popular;
(*above left*) a
prowling house
spider (*Herpyllus
blackwalli*);
(*above right*) a
garden spider
(*Araneus
diadematus*);
(*left*) a silver fish
(*Lepisma
saccharina*)

Page 72 (above) a hedgehog with young newly out of the nest. The hedgehog has successfully colonised the suburban gardens where it is usually regarded as the gardener's friend; (below) badgers are still fairly common around the outskirts of London

is the woodcock. In behaviour it is quite different from most other species, and its preferred habitat is dense woodland undergrowth. It is a bird which it is remarkably easy to overlook. During the breeding season it is a little more obvious, the display flight, known as 'roding', often drawing attention to the bird. In 1968 a woodcock was seen roding, and subsequently one of the park gamekeepers saw an adult bird with a young one. During the winter months the occasional woodcock can be flushed by the early morning visitor to the plantations.

The little information available on the life contained in the Pen Ponds dates mainly from the time when, during World War II, they were drained. Carp, bream, pike, perch, dace and eel were all taken from the ponds and, in the bottom, freshwater mussels were found, some nearly six inches long.

As pointed out earlier in this chapter, the separation of the Royal Parks is somewhat arbitrary and, in fact, one could make a very good case for dealing with the area of commons (Wimbledon, Ham, Sheen and Barnes commons and Putney Heath) as a single unit.

CHAPTER FIVE

London's other grasslands

Golf courses, playing fields, parks, airports—
Heaths and commons

APART FROM THE Royal Parks, scattered throughout London are
open spaces which consist basically of areas of grass—miniature
prairies of short closely cut turf. These include heaths, commons, playing fields, golf courses, airports and many of the
other parks. At one time wild and overgrown, many of the
heaths, commons and parks have been 'tidied' up so that a
motor mower can be taken over the grass. This, of course, has
far-reaching and, in the main, destructive effects. Those remaining are constantly under pressure from development schemes
of one sort or another. Many of the larger commons and heaths
have their own conservation or similar organisation, but the
vast majority of parks and open spaces are unprotected in this
way. A contrasting position seems to exist in another London—
in Ontario, Canada. There, with about 1,500 acres of park, they
claim to have more trees per person than any other city in the
world and, with a population of 200,000 and 400,000 official
trees, ie excluding privately owned ones, this claim seems justi-
fied. There are some 50 species and about 800 individual trees
are planted each year, local regulations ensuring that any new
development leaves room for such planting. Perhaps some of
London, England's, borough councils could bear this in mind.
Flat areas of grass are easy to maintain just as the mutilated
stumps which pass as lime trees are, but they are barely more
alive than a sheet of tarmac or a telegraph pole.

When discussing the wildlife of London's grasslands, as often
as not the absent species spring to mind as readily as those which

are present. So many species, such as the mole, should be there and yet do not occur. The mole is one of the few species of mammal which has almost completely failed to establish itself within the suburbs of London. There are isolated populations but they really are isolated and exceptional. The reason is a straightforward one—man and moles just cannot co-exist. Man does not want mole hills on his lawns or in neat lines across his football and cricket pitches, bowling greens, golf courses and so on. Since most of these amenities are on the outskirts of the metropolis, the mole is probably being pushed out more rapidly than any other animal.

GOLF COURSES, PLAYING FIELDS, PARKS, AIRPORTS

Within the grasslands covered by this heading golf courses, in some ways, represent a special case. They are a much more recent phenomenon than many people realise. The earliest golf course in London was one on Blackheath founded in about 1608, but the next ones appear to be those started at Wimbledon and Tooting Bec in the 1860s, and it was not until the 1880s that they really caught on. Just before World War II the number of golf courses had reached a peak, with somewhere in the region of 140 in the London area; since then the demand for land has meant that several suburban courses have disappeared.

Of the various types of 'grasslands', the golf courses probably have the richest fauna. This is because they also have the richest flora: an essential part of a good course are bunkers, copses and even ponds, and these provide cover for a wide variety of animals. In order to provide the obstacles and difficulties which a golfer requires many trees and shrubs, both native and introduced, have been planted. Often remarkable growths of gorse and broom, plants which seem to suffer considerably on common lands, are to be seen. The artificial sand dunes and bunkers sometimes provide a suitable habitat for plants normally found on coastal dunes; some of these such as marram grass *Ammophila arenaria* may be the result of deliberate planting, others such as sea milkwort *Glaux maritima* and sea plantain *Plantago maritima* may be accidentally introduced when turfing is in progress. Golf courses are often private and so marauding small boys, local inhabitants taking their dogs for walks and other forms of disturbance to flora and fauna are actively discouraged. One of the larger courses is at Dulwich, very near to the centre of London. This is in an ideal situation, being sandwiched between Dulwich Woods and Dulwich Park. The latter contains extensive grasslands, but also dense shrubberies of rhododendrons. The isolated clumps of hawthorn on the golf course provide breeding refuges for a number of birds, whose breeding success is noticeably higher than for birds along the edge of the nearby woods where the local lads can pillage the eggs. Nesting species on the golf course include crow, jay, magpie, bullfinch, linnet, goldfinch, skylark, great tit, blue tit and whitethroat.

Although golf courses may have the greater variety of successful breeding birds, the playing fields, parks and airports have the attraction of a wide selection of birds feeding on them particularly during the winter and whilst on migration. During the winter almost every suburban park, football pitch, golf course and any other sizeable lawn will have a regular population of feeding birds. These will be mainly thrushes, with a few finches, pigeons, starlings, gulls and crows. The thrushes are largely overlooked; how many of London's thousands of commuters even notice their existence as their train hurtles past scores of these birds each morning? Redwings, song thrushes, blackbirds, mistle thrushes and fieldfares all occur in varying proportions, on any suitable feeding ground. As far as I can ascertain no one as yet has studied how and why there is this variation so that, at different times of the year, there are more redwings than the rest of the species. It could be influenced by the weather, or it could be simply the size of the feeding area.

During the migration periods the open grassy slopes of parks and golf courses are ideal observation sites; tired migrants spot an area of open green, drop in for a few hours' rest, and are easily seen by the bird watcher. Primrose Hill was to become famous not only for the numbers of exciting birds seen there, but also because some years ago the ornithologist Ian Wallace realised that as well as these resting migrants there was an excellent vista, from the top of the hill, and that birds could actually be seen whilst migrating. Migration watches have since been carried out in many other places in London, often from the top of office blocks.

Whilst on migration, particularly during cold-weather movements, lapwings are a frequent visitor to the grasslands. Skylarks and meadow pipits often appear overnight in hundreds during a severe winter as do many of the finches such as greenfinches, linnets, chaffinches and even bramblings. These will often stay for up to several weeks, particularly if the prevailing weather in other parts of Britain is more severe. Wheatears, pipits and wagtails are passage migrants which can be expected to occur during spring or autumn on almost every sizeable stretch of grass in and around London. The other species of passage migrants should be looked for around the fringes of parks; they are not birds of open land, but are initially attracted by the overall greenness of the habitat. These birds include stonechats, whinchats and the occasional warbler. Apart from the regularly occurring migrants there is a long list of more exciting birds which turn up in small numbers each year. These include ring ouzel, pied flycatcher and hooded crow.

One of the notable features of the birdlife of the grasslands are the gulls in winter. The 'five' gulls (greater and lesser blackbacked, herring, common and black-headed) are all regular, though the common gull is often the least abundant! Although the numbers of gulls to be seen on playing fields are not nearly as vast as those encountered at the reservoirs where the gulls roost, they are of considerable interest, and much easier to deal with. The liking gulls have for flat areas of grass or even tarmac, has caused considerable difficulties at airports, not least at London's Heathrow and Gatwick. Bird-strikes, when an aircraft collides with a bird or flock of birds, can be very serious. A flock of black-backed gulls colliding with a jet plane as it takes off or lands can cause a considerable amount of damage. Each bird is fairly large, and a few of them going into the air-intake of a jet can easily foul it up. Recently many techniques for scaring them from airports have been tried and one which may spread to London's international airports, of particular interest to birdwatchers, involves the flying of falcons and hawks over the gulls to scare them into flight just before a plane takes off or lands.

London airport is close to Staines Moor and there is always a chance of seeing golden plover—a flock of around 250 usually winters on the moor.

HEATHS AND COMMONS

There are many commons scattered through the suburbs of London, particularly south of the Thames. They date from the times of the enclosure acts of the sixteenth century onwards, and were often poor quality land which was left to local commoners for grazing. On many of the commons the gravelly soils of the river terraces can be seen; it supports a poor, often a heathland, type of flora. Most such land has now been transformed into playing fields or planted extensively with both native and alien trees, but here and there small areas of the original heathland survive. The most famous, and most interesting to the naturalist, are probably Hampstead Heath and Wimbledon Common. (Putney Heath which adjoins Wimbledon Common is usually included in any description of the area.) Both Hampstead and Wimbledon are sufficiently overgrown to be of interest to naturalists, but there are many other areas worth a visit and, although in this chapter only Wimbledon is fully described, many of the general comments apply to other heaths and commons. Tooting and Graveney Commons, Streatham Common, Blackheath, Clapham Common and Wandsworth Common are just a few which, though considerably altered by man, are well worth a visit by naturalists who can study the natural history over a period of time, noting the changes that take place.

Adjoining Richmond Park are several small open spaces. The most interesting, to the naturalist, are Ham Common and East Sheen Common. Ham Common to the south-west is botanically interesting. At one time gorse and bracken were widespread, but a series of fires have reduced these plants. One of the most interesting species, which flowers in September, is the lesser water pepper *Polygonum minus*. Over the years many of the ditches and marshy areas have been filled by the dumping of garden refuse; this has introduced a wide variety of garden plants. Several older garden plants such as the star of Bethlehem *Ornithugalum umbellatum* and great celandine *Chelidonium majus* are to be found. Similarly, at one time, East Sheen Common was an area of heathland but fires, particularly that of 1921, and modern developments have encroached to a considerable extent. There is, however, some heather and gorse still existing, though the sundew once found there is unfortunately gone. Much of the common has now become playing fields, or is gradually becoming overgrown with trees.

Wimbledon Common

Wimbledon Common and Putney Heath, though wild and overgrown in appearance, are fairly modern in origin. They were not acquired for public use until 1871, and by that date they had been cleared of nearly all sizeable trees and were little more than waste ground. Since then they have been extensively planted with trees and are now well looked after. They are fairly typical and easily accessible from most parts of London and are described below in some detail.

The most frequently visited area of Wimbledon Common is the more open part in the south and east. Most of this area is situated on gravels and was until very recently largely bare of trees, but scrub and small trees are rapidly invading much of it. Immediately below the gravels lie the Claygate Beds—a stratum of sandy loam, which is exposed in the south-western part of the common. The rest of the common is on the heavy London Clay, which occurs below the Claygate Beds.

The flora of the common is, as might be expected from an area surrounded by suburbs, very varied and includes many introductions and escapes. The open grasslands, which are mainly on the gravels, are dominated by the purple moor grass *Molinia caerulea*, *Deschampia flexuosa*, *Festuca ovina* and ling *Calluna*. In the drier areas sheep's sorrel, heath bedstraw and related species are also found.

The woodlands contain a fascinating variety of species, in fact it has been suggested that if searched really thoroughly they would yield almost every species of tree native to Britain. Along Stag Lane at the south of the common is a good place to begin looking; here can be found several species of oak, both native and introduced. *Quercus palustria*, *Q. coccinea*, *Q. maxima*, *Q. robur* and *Q. cerris* have all been recorded. Probably the most widespread of the trees is the birch of which two species *Betula alba* and *B. verrucosa* occur, as well as hybrids. The birch is a rapidly growing species and is one of the first trees to colonise areas of scrub. It is also fairly short-lived and the rotting stumps provide a habitat for a wealth of insects and other invertebrates. In late autumn, in particular, extensive growths of fungi are noticeable growing on the birches and other trees and in the litter in the woods. The tawny grisette *Amanita fulva*, the milk mushroom *Lactarius rufus* and the suphur tuft *Hypholoma fascicular* are all fairly abundant and many other species occur in small numbers including the fly agaric the 'classic' toadstool, red with white spots and associated with gnomes throughout suburban areas.

Perhaps the most interesting flora is that which manages to linger on in the bogs and ponds. The marsh pennywort *Hydrocotyle vulgaris* is widespread in all the damp areas, and along the edges of the ponds it is worth looking for bur-marigold *Bidens tripartita*, lesser spearwort *Ranunculus flammula* and skullcap *Scutellaria galericulata*. The ponds also provide the entomologist with a good hunting ground—several species of dragonflies and damselflies occur together with many other insects.

Of the insects found on the common, the group most likely to attract attention are the butterflies. On a sunny day in summer a surprising variety can be seen. Small tortoiseshells and peacock butterflies are among the first to be seen on the wing and are likely to be encountered in the surrounding suburbs as they emerge from hibernation. One of the next species to emerge is the brimstone butterfly, but by late May or early June a much wider variety can be seen. The whites, large and small, are fairly common around the edge of the common and in the surrounding gardens. In the more sheltered parts of the common and even in the woods, the orange tip butterfly can be found. Both the holly blue and common blue occur but neither is particularly abundant. The small copper, green hairstreak, small skipper, painted lady, red admiral, small heath, speckled wood and meadow brown are just a few of the others likely to be encountered.

Of the mammals occurring on Wimbledon Common the most interesting are probably the fox and the badger, both of which also occur in some of the larger gardens nearby. The smaller mammals have not been at all well studied and very little is known about their distribution. In the past many animals, alas now lost, were recorded; the name of Beverley Brook which runs along the edge of the common commemorates the extinct beavers. Red squirrels were common earlier this century, and at one time natterjack toads bred. The birds are better observed and a regular visitor to the common could reckon on seeing eighty or more species in a year, though this would include many passage migrants. Most of the typical woodland birds occur, including lesser spotted woodpecker, blackcap, and garden warbler. Tree pipits breed in small numbers some years and cirl buntings are occasionally seen in the open scrub areas around the golf course. In winter quite large flocks of siskins and redpolls may be found, the latter in fact being present in small numbers in most months of the year. Large flocks of tits, including the long-tailed, also occur in winter.

An aspect of the past were the prehistoric earthworks, the most famous of which is known as Caesar's camp. In 1786 twenty-three small barrows and one large one were recorded near Tibbets Corner. These were gradually destroyed by being used to repair the parish roads. Tibbets Corner was the site of a recent earthworks—when the spoil from an underpass was dumped on the corner of Putney Heath.

CHAPTER SIX

London's artificial lakes

Reservoirs–Gravel pits

RESERVOIRS

IN WESTERN EUROPE the decline in the number of wetlands has been causing concern to ornithologists and ecologists for many years and, since to most of the 'civilised world' progress includes (or has done in the past) drainage of marshes and swamps and the pollution of rivers and lakes, reservoirs have become increasingly important to wild birds. As much of the water these reservoirs contain will be used for human consumption they are kept reasonably free of industrial pollution. The vast metropolis of London consumes an increasingly enormous quantity of water; the artificial lakes which store it provide a valuable habitat for a variety of birds. Most of the reservoirs in and around London are administered by the Metropolitan Water Board (MWB) and it is necessary to obtain a permit from this organisation in order to go birdwatching on their property. Permits are normally only granted to *bona fide* birdwatchers (evidence of this, such as membership of an ornithological society, is required) over twenty-one years of age.

There are a few reservoirs around London entirely unconnected with the MWB. Most of these were built to serve the canals; the Brent, or Welsh Harp, reservoir is the best-known example. The canal reservoirs usually have natural embankments along which grow willows, sallows, sedges and reeds. Unlike the MWB ones they are often used for recreational purposes such as sailing or even water skiing. The birds attracted to canal reservoirs will be slightly different on account of the richer vegetation; however, to most species of bird the purpose for which man has collected the water is unimportant, a bird sees and is attracted by a large expanse of water.

The reservoirs are of relatively recent origin. In 1835 there were only three, all for feeding canals—the Brent, Aldenham and Ruislip. By the time J. E. Harting was writing about birds in the second half of the nineteenth century, the total area of the reservoirs, including small ones at Walthamstow and Barnes, was only about 200 acres. By 1900 this acreage had more than doubled and the reservoirs formed an important series of large artificial lakes. Birds at one time considered rare in London suddenly found a home. At the present time the London reservoirs are amongst the most important birdwatching areas in the British Isles. They are also among the most closely observed. Any bird which pauses around Staines reservoir, for example, for more than a few minutes during the spring or autumn migration has little chance of passing unnoticed.

There are two main groups of reservoirs: those situated in the Lea Valley, ie Walthamstow, King George V and William Girling reservoirs; secondly the Thames Valley reservoirs, the largest of which are Barn Elms, Island Barn, Queen Elizabeth II, Queen Mary, King George VI and Staines.

Birds

Staines reservoir is one of the most popular with birdwatchers because of the wide variety of species which visit it. Access is easy since almost all the birds can be seen from the public footpath on the causeway which divides the two halves of the reservoir.

During the winter months vast numbers of waterfowl can be seen; most abundant are mallard, teal, wigeon, tufted duck and pochard. Other species usually present, though in smaller numbers, include shoveler, goldeneye, smew and goosander. During most winters pintail and red-breasted merganser occur, but somewhat erratically. The ducks are the most noticeable birds but other waterfowl are also present. Cormorants—usually associated with coastal waters in the British Isles—are conspicuous. Coot are numerous and various species of divers occur regularly. The grebes and divers often pose a considerable problem in identification. Staines, for instance, is a fairly large reservoir and a grebe or diver continually submerging and reappearing several hundred yards away is difficult to see, let alone identify. But the beginner need not worry too much at Staines, the chances are that there will be several other birdwatchers around to help with any tricky observation. Great crested grebes are present throughout the year and red-necked, black-necked and Slavonian grebes are recorded most winters. Most of the birds listed above occur also at the other reservoirs, if not regularly then in small numbers during hard weather or on migration. As wintering grounds the reservoirs are extremely important. Each year an International Wildfowl Count is held and in 1969, out of a total of 64 smew recorded in Britain, 49 were on London reservoirs— 17 on Staines and 32 on Brent.

The reservoirs are used by gulls as roosting grounds and the number flying in each evening has been steadily increasing over many years. Bryan Sage in a study of the roosting populations found that in 1963 there were about 220,500 gulls roosting on the London reservoirs and that by 1968 this number had risen to about 265,700. The reservoir holding the largest population was the Queen Elizabeth II, with somewhere in the region of 100,000 gulls. The most abundant species was the black-headed gull which accounted for more than 165,000 of the 1968 total; other gulls included in this census were common, herring, greater black-backed and lesser black-backed. Little gulls occasionally occur on the reservoirs, particularly Staines, and kittiwakes may be seen most years. Glaucous and Iceland gulls are a possibility although they are more often seen on rubbish tips.

During the migration seasons of spring and autumn, terns occur at some of the reservoirs; Staines is once again probably the best locality. Black terns are regular passage migrants and a sharp eye may detect a white-winged black tern. 'Commic' terns (jargon for common/Arctic terns) are abundant at Staines, and a few can be found at most of the other reservoirs. In late autumn Staines is particularly well known for black-necked grebes, the maximum number usually being somewhere around 10, though in 1945 a flock of 21 was recorded—a record as yet unbeaten.

Probably the nearest reservoirs to central London are those at Stoke Newington. A bare four miles from St Pauls, they consist of two small pools. During a severe winter they can provide interesting bird sights as, being situated well towards the centre of London, they are slightly later in freezing over on account of the generally warmer climate of the built-up area. When the main reservoirs are frozen Stoke Newington comes into its own and large numbers of birds may move in. Tufted duck, pochard, smew and great-crested grebe can all be expected, and probably several other species. In the winter of 1969–70 up to 650 pochard and 2,000 tufted duck were recorded with a maximum of 18 smew.

During mid-summer the reservoirs are a favourite feeding locality for swifts and hirundines (swallows and martins) which often gather in very large flocks. Pied wagtails as well as several other species are often found breeding alongside the water, but it is the waterfowl and gulls which are truly characteristic of such a habitat.

What is it that makes the reservoirs such an attractive place for birds? The gulls look for a large expanse of open water on which to roost. The modern deep, steep-sided reservoirs are ideal. They are not capable of supporting a growth of rooted plants but algae and some floating plants can thrive. One of the most abundant species of algae is *Fragilaria crotonensis* which arrives at the reservoirs via the Thames. Since the Thames, which supplies the reservoirs, is full of organic matter it is not surprising that very high concentrations of algae are often seen. The diving ducks such as pochard, tufted duck and goldeneye feed on the molluscs, insect larvae and worms which live mainly at the bottom of the reservoirs, and for this reason they are most abundant on the older, shallower reservoirs such as those at Barn Elms.

Fish

Fish also play a part in the ecology of the reservoirs. They have been introduced into some, but detailed records are lacking. Barn Elms is known to contain roach, perch and ruff. Eels probably occur in most, but the only published records are from West Molesey, Staines and Queen Mary reservoirs. The roach is one of the most widespread recorded species and as well as at Barn Elms, has been observed at Staines, Queen Mary, Littleton and West Molesey. The other species recorded from London reservoirs are bronze bream, ruff, gudgeon and golden orfe. This list is obviously well short of the truth and would provide an ideal subject for some fairly straightforward research. Some of the reservoirs allow anglers to fish the waters, and by inspecting their catch the contents of the reservoir could easily be determined.

Molluscs and other invertebrates

Among the more spectacular colonists of the reservoirs is the zebra mussel *Dreissena polymorpha*. It was first found in the Surrey Commercial Docks in 1824. By 1840 the naturalist J. E. Gray observed that it was 'to be found in most of the docks communicating with the Thames' and he considered that it had been introduced with imported timber from the Volga. By the 1860s it was widespread in London's waterways and often caused considerable inconvenience. One of the largest 'infestations' was that recorded in 1912 when 90 tons of mussels were cleaned out from a water-main; originally this had been 3ft in diameter but the mussels had reduced the effective diameter to 9in. The zebra mussel is not normally recorded away from the Thames Valley and the Lea Valley river and reservoir systems.

Other aquatic animals found in the reservoirs include sponges, hydroids, a wide variety of insect larvae, worms and other invertebrates. A somewhat bizarre animal collected in the reservoirs is a small crustacean *Niphargus*. This species is a blind shrimp and has colonised the pipes beneath the reservoir filters where the habitat is similar to the caves where such species are normally found. Perhaps the blind salamander *Proteus* of the Balkan countries could be introduced!

GRAVEL PITS

During construction reservoirs are remarkably similar to gravel pits and a gravel pit, once its useful life is over, is often filled with water and acquires several characteristics in common with reservoirs. It is therefore logical to deal with both these habitats under the same chapter heading.

Gravel pits, like reservoirs, are a relatively modern occurrence. The advent of concrete for major construction work meant that large quantities of sands and gravels were needed and, soon after World War I, such extraction industry began to expand rapidly. Gravel pits may be found wherever the gravelly stratas occur, and in the London area these are most abundant in west Middlesex. Once gravel pits have been exhausted and allowed to fill with water, in a very short time they become overgrown with a wide variety of plants particularly sallows, willows, great reedmace and a variety of sedges, rushes and other aquatic flora. The embankments are colonised by willow herbs, ragworts and other plants familiar on bombed sites and waste ground throughout London. Within a few years a sturdy growth of trees takes over, the vegetation becomes settled and well established.

Gravel pits are also extremely interesting while they are actually being worked or when they have only recently fallen into disuse, for it is then that the little ringed plover, one of Britain's rarest breeding birds, nests. This species is fairly common as a breeding bird on the mainland of Europe, but in Britain it is almost entirely restricted to gravel pits and

Page 89 (above) House martins have long been linked with man—in fact cliff nesting sites are now rather rare; (below) the ubiquitous house sparrow has probably declined in London since horse-drawn traffic disappeared

Page 90 At the turn of this century gulls were not common visitors to many parts of London. Now they are abundant and often tame, particularly black-headed gulls

reservoirs under construction, some twenty to twenty-five pairs breeding each year in the London area. Because of the little ringed plover's rarity the actual sites are not normally disclosed and, since they are also usually on privately owned property, the bird's future is fairly safe—but no more than fairly safe. Protection from egg collectors and even over-enthusiastic bird-watchers is comparatively straightforward, but habitat protection is not quite that simple. If the little ringed plovers nest in gravel pits which are still worked there is an obvious risk of the eggs being destroyed; if the nests are in pits which have only recently fallen into disuse, the danger is that such pits usually flood or become rapidly overgrown and, in a couple of years, are unsuitable for nesting. When reservoirs are drained for cleaning they too provide a suitable nesting habitat; when one of the Walthamstow reservoirs was drained in 1970 three pairs of little ringed plovers and a pair of ringed plovers nested there.

Another bird which is often found nesting in pits which are still being operated is the sand martin. This species is a colonial nester which excavates tunnels into sandy cliffs and banks. The sand martin has even managed to adapt to an urban environment in some places by nesting in pipes, an interesting occurrence which has been observed in London.

The habitat provided by an overgrown and flooded gravel pit is exceptionally rich. This in its turn attracts a wide variety of birds. Common sandpipers have bred in the Lea Valley gravel pits and redshank breed at pits all round London. Common terns breed in small numbers at Broxbourne Pit. The dense vegetation of sallow and reeds such as *Phragmites* which rapidly grow along the edges of disused pits is soon colonised by many species of small birds such as reed buntings, sedge warblers and reed warblers. During the winter the gravel pits have a bird fauna similar to the reservoirs but it is on a smaller scale and often with a more interesting variety. Grebes, ducks and coot are all found there together with passerine birds in the surrounding bushes and trees. Many other birds may also be observed by the alert naturalist.

F

The decline in the number of natural ponds in many parts of London has led to a decline in amphibians: toads, frogs and newts have in many places become quite rare. It is possible that if they can manage to gain a hold in the gravel pits they may be able to survive although, generally speaking, amphibians prefer smaller areas of water.

Gravel pits are a useful laboratory for a naturalist, for there colonisation by plants and animals can be accurately and thoroughly studied. It is a task which few naturalists have in fact carried out.

CHAPTER SEVEN

Sewage farms and rubbish tips

Rubbish through the ages—Sewage farms—
Rubbish tips

REFUSE AND RUBBISH can be one of the most interesting aspects of the natural history of a city. As soon as man settles there or in a town or even a village, the disposal of waste matter becomes a problem. Since the Industrial Revolution the quality of the waste has greatly changed; factory waste and the steady increase in the amount of tins, paper and other types of packaging have created enormous problems in refuse disposal. In the past the problem was to a large extent left to the individual, and it was not until the mid-nineteenth century that Londoners began to develop efficient sewage and refuse disposal systems.

RUBBISH THROUGH THE AGES

During the Roman occupation of Britain, London, as an important centre, would have had well-planned systems for dealing with waste. But soon after the departure of the Romans from Britain the efficient cities they had created declined so that during the Middle Ages the vast majority of the densely packed mass of humanity in London lived under what would be today described as thoroughly unhygienic conditions. Most of the rivers and ditches running through London were little more than open sewers, frequently blocked by refuse. The resulting stagnant quagmires were infested with mosquitoes, carriers of malaria, then known as the 'ague'. Nearly all these water courses have now been covered and incorporated into the general drainage system; the only reminder of these old brooks, bournes and ditches is to be found in such place names as Wallbrook, Tyburn and Houndsditch. For centuries the waterways were used as sewers and the disposal of solid refuse was left to scavengers, human or otherwise. Not until 1737 was the River Fleet covered over—an act long overdue judging by contemporary descriptions of its stench.

During the early part of the Middle Ages pigs were encouraged as scavengers, but the herds of semi-wild swine became a menace and so later they were discouraged. The other scavenging mammals of medieval London probably included house mice, polecats and semi-wild cats and dogs. An unwelcome addition to this fauna was the black rat, which animal was to have a considerable effect on the city, becoming an important member of London's fauna. Its usefulness as a scavenger is small when compared with the damage it can inflict on man and his property. The exact date when the black rat arrived in Britain is unknown although many writers state that it was carried in the ships of crusaders returning from the Levant; there is, in fact, very little evidence to support this theory. Written records have to be treated with extreme caution and there is hardly any archaeological evidence.

In 1348 over half the population of London died in the 'Black Death', a form of plague usually transmitted by a flea *Xenopsylla cheopis* which is common on rats. The 'Black Death' is often cited as the best evidence for the presence of rats in England at that time, but the facts do not entirely support this theory. The plague flea is known from many other hosts, and other species of flea such as the common human flea *Pulex irritans* as well as lice and ticks are all able to carry the plague in the absence of rats. The plague of 1665 carried off over 90,000 people and a reminder of it is to be seen in the raised levels of many of the city churchyards.

London, from at least medieval times onwards, has had its

scavenging birds. Jackdaws nested throughout London and continued to nest in numbers in Kensington Gardens until 1957 and on several occasions since. In the past they must have been familiar scavengers together with ravens, kites and carrion crows, the latter so closely associated with scavenging that even its name reflects the habit. Until the custom of displaying the heads of felons and traitors over London Bridge was discontinued, kites and ravens were a common sight hovering close by. The raven managed to survive in London until the mid-nineteenth century, which is surprising when we consider how restricted its range is now. According to W. H. Hudson, the last pair of ravens to nest in central London nested in Hyde Park in 1826, but they survived around the outskirts of London until 1845, when the last pair nested near Enfield. Hudson also records the last kites' nest in London—in 1777 in Gray's Inn gardens. The identity of the kites which used to be so common around London has never been conclusively settled; the black kite has never been proved to have bred in this country but is known as a scavenger and commensal in other parts of Europe, whereas the red kite is known to have been quite common in many parts of the British Isles but is not usually as gregarious as the black kite.

By the end of the eighteenth century kites were no longer to be seen flying over London but a new scavenger had arrived. This was the brown rat. (Both the black rat and brown rat are extremely variable in colour, in fact black 'brown rats' and brown 'black rats' are common.) The exact date of the arrival of the brown rat will probably never be known, but it was near enough to the arrival of George I for them to be dubbed by some people the 'Hanoverian rat'. Charles Waterton (1782-1865), a famous eccentric and naturalist, like many of his contemporaries linked the two events and in the 1850s he wrote: 'this brute like the family which first brought it over exists in round numbers and demands a most plentiful supply of food'. It is difficult to decide which he detested most, the rats or the royal family!

The metropolis as we know it now, was beginning to develop during the nineteenth century. The problems of waste disposal had become so acute by around the 1850s that a public waste disposal system was organised. Nowadays instead of refuse and raw sewage being emptied into the rivers, most of the refuse is taken to 'tips' and much of the sewage is processed on sewage 'farms', usually situated on the outskirts of the metropolis. The twentieth-century scavenger is no longer the raven or kite but the gull (see Rubbish tips, page 103).

(see Rubbish tips, page 103)

SEWAGE FARMS

Non-birdwatchers usually raise their eyebrows in amazement when they first learn of a birdwatcher's addiction to visiting sewage farms. These sites, however, are among the best localities in the London area for birdwatching as the methods by which the sewage is processed involves the formation of large areas of artificial marshland, which attracts migrating waders and waterfowl to interrupt their spring and autumn migrations for a brief rest. The most widely known farms such as Rye Meads, Hersham, Perry Oaks and Beddington are watched regularly by birdwatchers and the results can be very rewarding, as a brief look at a copy of the annual *London Bird Report* will show. Apart from the occasional rarities, every year hundreds of the commoner wading birds are seen on sewage farms around London. Ruff, ringed plover, jack snipe, curlew, whimbrel, spotted redshank, golden plover and many other species are seen regularly and each year a few species of marshland birds, such as redshank, snipe and yellow wagtail nest there.

The marshes and lagoons of sewage farms provide excellent breeding sites for a wide variety of flies. Some of the commonest of these are the non-biting midges which often gather in very large swarms and from a distance resemble a column of smoke. Many insect-eating birds are attracted by the vast numbers of flies, notably swifts, swallows and martins; swifts in particular often travel long distances in order to feed on the high concentration of insects. The water meadows and fringes provide interesting mammals and plants.

The sewage farms of interest to naturalists, such as Rye Meads, Beddington, Perry Oaks, and Hersham all have different characteristics, but the basic principles of their working are the same. Raw sewage effluent arrives at the farm and is broken down by the use of bacteria. After many filtering processes the result is a large quantity of sludge and a vast quantity of water. In the past—and still, on a few farms—the final filtering of the water was done by flooding water meadows and allowing the water to run off. Now the sludge is pumped into large lagoons and left to dry out, when it is usually sold as fertiliser. In the earliest sewage farms, crops were grown on the very fertile soils of the farm and the water meadows were used for fattening cattle. Unfortunately this type of sewage farm, so attractive to naturalists, is about to disappear. They are large—Beddington is 600 acres—and the demand for land around London is always increasing. Over the next few years it is probable that many of them will either be closed down or will at least contract in size as they become mechanised.

Beddington sewage farm

Since the author was connected with the bird-ringing station which operates at Beddington sewage farm, Surrey, its natural history will be taken as being fairly characteristic of present sewage farms in general although it is, at the time of writing, in a state of change from the old-style farm to a new mechanised sewage-processing works. Even with the absence of its former water meadows and consequent reduction in the number of fields, hedgerows and trees, it will provide a surprising variety of habitats. The lagoons for drying sludge are formed by bull-dozing earth embankments and then pumping the sludge into them. The sludge takes many weeks to dry and attracts different types of wildlife. As would be expected this rich, wet habitat provides a breeding ground for an enormous variety of insects, particularly flies. Not only is the variety interesting but the actual numbers are often vast. By far the most numerous order is Diptera (flies), with Coleoptera (beetles) and Hymenoptera (ants, bees and wasps) also prominent. The wet marshland of the flooded grassfields provides a breeding ground for a wide variety of species of non-biting midges belonging to the family Chironomidae and also for *Sepsidae*, *Ptychoptera*, *Eristalis tenax* and *Scatophaga*. These latter species are normally only found in aquatic habitats with a rich organic content, which sewage farms provide. When a sewage farm is functioning normally the insects play an important part in the filtering processes, but occasionally they may have adverse effects.

The aphid *Aphis gossypi* sometimes occurs in plague proportions on grasses such as the sweet grass *Glyceria plicata*. This aphid often introduces a virus which attacks the grass turning it brown and brittle, and ultimately destroying large areas of it. Unfortunately the insect fauna of grass plots on these sewage farms has not been extensively studied, yet it is a habitat worthy of the attention of entomologists before it is entirely superceded by more modern methods of purification.

The long grass of the water meadows provides an abundant food supply for short-tailed voles. The population of these animals is cyclical and similar to the more famous lemmings— every few years a 'plague' occurs. In these plague years the voles seem to be everywhere. Not unexpectedly their large numbers attract predators. Foxes are always present at Beddington—as on most of the other sewage farms—and are able to rear above-average numbers of litters. The birds of prey are also prolific. Kestrels have a successful breeding season and very often short-eared owls are attracted to the farm in winter. As recently as the end of 1970, up to eight short-eared owls were feeding on the voles at Beddington.

The flora of sewage farms is normally only of interest around the fringes, ie along hedgerows and paths. Some groups, such as the lichens, are however of outstanding interest. J. R. Laundon recently studied the lichen flora of Beddington sewage farm and found twenty-one species, mainly on the concrete of the carrier dykes. Three of the species recorded are not known from anywhere else in the London area.

Swifts, swallows and martins are, as already mentioned, characteristic of sewage farms in summer, feeding on the myriads of aphids, midges and other insects which are so abundant. The swift, in particular, has been studied at several of the sewage farms around London, as well as on the reservoirs where they also congregate. The ringing stations at Beddington, Hersham, and Rye Meads, and the now defunct groups at Elmers End and Epsom sewage farms, have between them ringed large numbers. Beddington is the most important of these stations, and has been ringing swifts every year since 1956; now nearly 10,000 have been marked. From the recoveries of birds found dead, together with details of those caught by other ringers, much has been learned about the life of a suburban swift. The recoveries show that they migrate down the west of Europe, through France, Spain and Morocco, to winter in the Congo; this has been confirmed by recoveries of birds ringed in other parts of Britain. It has also been possible to reconstruct a rough idea of the breeding distribution of swifts in and around London; they have fairly large feeding areas, and may travel up to eight miles to a good feeding ground. They show a preference for older houses, but this may be because they are not expanding their range. From ringing swifts it has also been possible to show that the young birds set off for Africa almost as soon as they have fledged. Since it is also thought that they rarely attempt to nest in their first year it is possible that, once they leave the nest, they may stay on the wing for eighteen months or more—a remarkable feat.

Rye Meads

Situated on the outskirts of suburban London, Rye Meads and the adjacent sewage farm have become well known on account of the intensive studies, made by the Rye Meads Ringing Group, of the birds in the area. The results have been published in the *London Bird Report* for 1963. The main part of the sewage farm consists of lagoons, the largest of which are several hundred yards across. Between the lagoons and the River Lea, which runs along one side, is an area of marshland. Waterfowl and many other birds nest in the overgrown edges of the lagoons and nearby ditches, but the main interest to ornithologists is in the visiting birds. Many migrants pass through and others, such as swifts, swallows and martins feed over the lagoons during the summer. These species and many others are trapped for ringing and studied in detail.

The species, typical of the habitat, which breed most years include great-crested and little grebes, tufted duck, reed and sedge warblers and yellow wagtail. The birds occurring on passage include a variety of waders, the following being recorded most years: little ringed plover, snipe, jack snipe, green sandpiper, common sandpiper, redshank and dunlin. Several other species have been recorded including rarities such as the solitary sandpiper. Common terns occur throughout the summer, probably being birds from the small colony which breeds nearby at Broxbourne gravel pits. The largest numbers of waterfowl usually occur in late autumn, when the most abundant species are mallard (700 or more) tufted duck and coot (about 100 of each); and pochard (up to 50). Shoveler, wigeon and teal also occur in small numbers.

The Rye Meads Ringing Group's report also includes notes on other aspects of the natural history of Rye Meads. In 1970 L. Lloyd-Evans compiled a list of the mollusca recorded and found that over 40 per cent of the British molluscan fauna was present. Of the 72 species recorded, 31 were aquatic, 11 amphibians and the remainder terrestrial. One of the most interesting species recorded was *Succinea elegans*, but this species is exceptionally difficult to identify; it is necessary to dissect the animal to determine its identity accurately. Lloyd-Evans regards the wandering snail *Lymnea peregra* as one of the most ecologically important species as it occurs in large numbers and provides food for tufted duck, pochard, great-crested grebe, little grebe and coot. It is the most abundant and widespread freshwater gastropod in the British Isles.

Birdwatchers see the occasional mammal and members of the ringing group have analysed owl pellets and undertaken live-trapping programmes. The common, pygmy and water shrews all occur, the water shrew being the most frequently observed. This is probably because not only is it the largest species of shrew, but it is also more conspicuous in its behaviour—it can be seen swimming and diving after aquatic insects and other small animals.

The water shrew could possibly be confused with the water vole, which also occurs at Rye Meads, but the vole is larger with a blunt muzzle, whereas that of the shrew is pointed. As the water shrew swims and dives it seems to be a glistening bubble with a nose, tail and scurrying legs sticking out. This bubble-like appearance comes from the air which is trapped in the short velvety fur. On land the movements of the water shrew are hurried and erratic, in contrast to the water vole which will usually potter along the embankments of rivers and ditches. The brown rat also occurs at Rye Meads, and will frequently take to the water. Unlike the water vole, the brown rat normally swims with the body only half submerged, and the long tail trailing behind is conspicuous.

Bank voles and wood mice occur in small numbers and, judging from the results of owl pellet analysis, field voles are abundant. The diminutive harvest mouse is also present in small numbers. In the older natural history books the harvest mouse was always regarded as an inhabitant of cornfields and for many years it was believed that it was declining—the combine harvester was often blamed. Naturalists believed it to be more or less extinct around London but fairly recently it was found that, whilst by no means common, it was by no means as rare as formerly believed. But few, if any, of the colonies around London are in cornfields. They were found to be mainly living in overgrown ditches. The best time to search is mid-winter as at this time the vegetation has died down and the nests, a mass of grasses about the size of a cricket ball, are clearly visible attached to half-a-dozen grass or sedge stems some eighteen inches or two feet above the ground.

Rabbits and hares both occur at Rye Meads and are preyed on by foxes, stoats and weasels; but only the latter is seen at all frequently. On a summer evening as the last of the swifts, swallows and martins are flying off to roost, bats come to Rye Meads to feed on the abundant supply of flying insects. Bats are almost impossible to identify in flight, but so far members of the ringing group have managed to mist-net four species: pipistrelle, long-eared, noctule and serotine. These four species can just about be picked out as they fly around Rye Meads. The pipistrelle is the smallest bat, but can easily be confused with other species such as whiskered and Daubenton's, which may one day be shown to occur. The long-eared hunts around trees, often hovering, and the ears can be clearly seen. The only species this bat is likely to be confused with are rare. The largest bats, noctule and serotine, can be distinguished fairly accurately in flight: the noctule has more pointed wings than the serotine and a rather erratic flight, frequently 'corkscrewing' towards the ground from a considerable height. The serotine, with its more rounded wings, has a much steadier motion.

In 1973, as part of the large-scale plans to turn the Lea Valley into a recreational zone for Londoners, the Royal Society for the Protection of Birds opened a small seventeen-acre bird reserve at Rye Meads, adjacent to the sewage farm. Unlike most bird reserves, there are no rarities breeding, but there is a good selection of interesting residents and migrants and the main function of this reserve will be in providing facilities for local naturalists, particularly children. Already, by making rafts on the sewage lagoons, common terns have started to breed, and by careful management it is hoped that many other wetland species will do the same.

RUBBISH TIPS

Solid refuse is removed from our dustbins at regular intervals by the local council dustmen and taken to rubbish tips or dumped at sea. Like the sewage farms most of the rubbish tips are situated on the outskirts of London and have a distinctive fauna. In his study of such dumps in the London area, A. Gibbs found that the most frequent bird visitors were gulls, crows, house sparrows, starlings, feral pigeons, kestrels and pied wagtails. Sometimes the numbers of birds feeding on a dump are large: up to 4,000 black-headed gulls have been recorded at Holywell Hyde dump and up to 250 carrion crows and 150 jackdaws at Charlton tip.

Among the many other animals found in large numbers on rubbish tips are brown rats and house crickets. The crickets are most active at dusk, when their chirping can be heard for a considerable distance, attracting bats and in particular the noctule bat. A few of these animals of London's waste tips are encouraged, most are branded as 'pests' or 'vermin', and ruthlessly hunted and destroyed.

The gulls are a striking example of how rapidly some animals can adapt to the 'un-natural' environment of a city. They congregate not only on rubbish tips, but also on the sewage farms. A flock of about 1,200 lesser black-backed gulls have been seen on Hersham sewage farm, only twenty-five acres in extent.

In the nineteenth century, gulls replaced crows and kites as the scavenging birds of the city. During the first decades of the present century first black-headed gulls, then common and herring gulls were regular visitors to London, though not in large numbers. The greater and lesser black-backed gulls were rare. By the late 1920s the numbers of gulls seen each year had begun to rise and at the present time all five species of gull mentioned above are seen in large numbers in London. Their numbers continue to rise, as B. Sage has shown in his counts of gulls roosting on reservoirs. In 1953 he estimated that there were about 85,000 gulls roosting on the larger reservoirs in the

London area, many of which feed on sewage farms and rubbish tips. Ten years later he estimated that the number of gulls roosting on the same reservoirs was approximately 221,000

In recent years gulls have also nested in London. The black-headed gull was the first to establish itself as a breeding species. They nested on Perry Oaks sewage farm, next to London Airport, up to 300 nests being built safe from most predators in the middle of one of the sludge tanks. The first nests were found in 1946 and breeding went on successfully until, unexpectedly, in 1962 the number of nests dropped to forty and at the time of writing they no longer nest. Recently herring gulls, attracted by the captive gulls, have bred successfully next to one of the large aviaries in London Zoo in Regent's Park. Lesser black-backed gulls have also bred.

Interesting though rubbish tips are, most naturalists are only too aware of the problems of pollution that such waste disposal creates. The average man produces around 600 to 700lb of rubbish each year; and the Greater London Council has to dispose of something over 4 million tons of rubbish in the same period. This gives an indication of the size and seriousness of the problem. The rubbish tips are soon to be a thing of the past. In a modern refuse disposal unit the rubbish is emptied on to conveyor belts and sieved for ashes and dirt to be used in road making or brick making; an electromagnet is passed over it to extract ferrous metals; it is hand sorted to remove glass as well as any saleable items; finally it is incinerated at temperatures of around 1,000° C.

In August 1970 the GLC opened its new disposal plant at Edmonton. It cost £10 million and is capable of dealing with about 1,300 tons of rubbish a day or nearly 500,000 tons a year. The incinerating furnaces are used to drive steam turbines producing electricity which will be used in the plant; any excess will be sold to the national grid. This sale of electricity is expected to raise about £500,000 a year. The cooling systems and filtration of the gases is by using purified sewage effluent. No rubbish tips for wildlife but a much better environment.

CHAPTER EIGHT

The green belt

Bookham Common—Box Hill and the North Downs—Harefield Great Pit—Epping Forest

THE GREEN BELT of London was established in 1938 when building was prohibited by Act of Parliament in the area beyond the suburban ring and, shortly after World War II, the Town & Country Planning Act rendered it necessary to obtain permission for any new building to be erected. The result has been a fairly effective halt in the growth of London during the last thirty years, in certain directions. The green belt is composed partly of rural agricultural land and partly of recreational land, private or public. The large public recreational areas include some of exceptional interest to naturalists, such as Epping Forest to the north-east, and the National Trust areas of Box Hill and the surrounding country to the south. The green belt preserves much of the wildlife that at one time could be found throughout many other parts of London, though even here it is often impoverished. The levels of pollution in the atmosphere and the rivers are, on the whole, lower in the green belt and, due to public outcry, the use of agricultural pesticides has been curtailed and is far less of a menace to wildlife, though the danger is still present.

The advent of the motor car, and its gradual rise to power has had a considerable effect on wildlife, particularly in the green belt. The greater mobility of London's population has increased the pressures on places far away from London. None the less one must also remember that this greater mobility has probably given the public a greater awareness of wildlife too, a circumstance reflected in the rise in demand for National Parks and Nature Reserves as the pressure of urban population increases.

There are many fine places in the green belt surrounding London for a naturalist to explore; the already mentioned Epping Forest and Boxhill, Hainault Forest, Lullingstone Park, Limpsfield Common, Bookham Common and numerous others.

BOOKHAM COMMON

For nearly thirty years members of the London Natural History Society (LNHS) have been surveying Bookham Common in detail. The interest from a naturalist's point of view lies in this detailed knowledge of the area. Each year reports on the research in progress are given in the *London Naturalist* and recently a well equipped research centre was opened by members of the LNHS, who will always give a warm welcome to visiting naturalists. The survey work is normally carried out on the first Sunday of the month, though other visits are also arranged.

The vegetation of the common has been thoroughly studied and at the present time nearly 500 species of flowering plants, 75 species of lichen and almost 250 species of fungi are known to occur there. The area consists mainly of woodlands in which the dominant tree is the oak *Quercus robur*, open plains of grasses where *Deschampsia caespitosa* and *Molinia caerulea* are predominant, large areas dominated by bracken *Pteridium aquilinum* and scrub areas. There are also several interesting marshy areas, ponds and flooded bomb craters.

The eastern plain was at one time a typical wet heathland, but in recent years birch, aspen and bracken have encroached on this area, and the dense growth of bracken has reduced the heathland flora to a few scattered remnants. In 1969 an attempt was made to conserve it by cutting back the bracken. The scheme was apparently a success. The Bayfield Plain and Central Plain were until 1969 being invaded and dominated by the coarse grass *Deschampia caespitosa* and subsequently by hawthorn. The cutting back of some of the *Deschampia* allowed the growth of

Page 107 (*above*) Tufted ducks breed in many of the central London parks, but they are most abundant on the reservoirs, where they occur in large numbers in winter; (*below*) the mute swan is a popular ornamental bird found on many larger lakes and ponds in and around London. In summer the Dyers and Vintners Companies go swan 'upping' on the Thames, when young swans are marked to show ownership

Page 108 (*above*) The wood pigeon is normally a very shy and wary bird, but in London it has overcome its fear of man and nests wherever there are a few trees; (*below*) herring gulls, attracted by the inmates of the aviaries, have recently taken to nesting in Regent's Park Zoo

a more interesting flora of rushes, *Juncus* species, on the Bayfield Plain, and on the Central Plain the umbellifer *Angelica sylvestris* now flourishes.

Over 300 species of butterflies and moths (excluding 'micros') have been recorded from the common, and over 1,200 species of flies. Many other insect groups have been studied there intensively and, as a result, several new species have been discovered. Over 600 species of beetles, 150 species of heteropterous bugs, 16 species of dragonflies and 12 species of Orthoptera (grasshoppers, bush crickets, etc) have been recorded. Extensive work on plant-galls has been carried out and well over 200 species have been recorded.

An annual census has been made of the bird population and any changes in this are noted. Woodcock breed most years, but they are difficult birds to locate except when performing their display flight. In spring the beautiful though somewhat monotonous song of the nightingale is one of the features of Bookham. The mechanical-sounding song of the grasshopper warbler, usually likened to a fishing reel being wound on a ratchet, is also characteristic. Redpolls also nest on the more open parts of the common. Birds typical of woodland and scrub such as nuthatch, marsh tit, long-tailed tit, chiffchaff, willow warbler, garden warbler, blackcap, whitethroat and yellowhammer all breed there.

An interesting recent arrival is the mandarin duck. During the last few years this species has been steadily spreading along the Mole Valley, which it colonised from its original point of introduction in Windsor Great Park and Virginia Water. The Isle of Wight ponds, with the woodlands growing close to the water's edge, are an ideal habitat for this bizarre looking duck which nests in holes in trees. It is breeding fairly regularly on Bookham Common and is quite easily seen. During the winter up to thirty have been recorded.

Roe deer have been seen on several occasions, the best time being in winter when the vegetation dies off. A kid has also been observed and thus it seems likely that they have bred on the

G

common. Grey squirrels are abundant, as are rabbits when myxomatosis is not rife. Of the carnivores the shy nocturnal badger and numerous foxes occur. Weasels are fairly frequently seen, but the smaller mammals need to be searched for carefully. Around the ponds, dustbins and railway embankments, discarded bottles, buried in the undergrowth and overlooked by the keepers, may provide a clue to the small mammals found on the common (see Appendix Three). The following species have all been found at Bookham: pygmy, common and water shrews, bank and field (short-tailed) vole, wood mouse, harvest mouse and dormouse. The last two are rare. The small mammals have also been studied by examining the pellets of birds of prey and also by live trapping, with Longworth traps.

The several ponds on Bookham Common present an interesting problem in conservation; if left to themselves they become overgrown and eventually so choked with sallows that no open water is left. If the ponds are cleaned out, this obviously has a very disturbing effect, even if it is only temporary, and it may be several years before the natural balance returns to normal. At one time a number of the bomb craters provided habitats very similar to dew ponds, but most of these are now either completely overgrown or heavily polluted with oil and rusting metal from old bicycles, petrol drums and various other refuse dumped in them.

In the spring the ponds are a good locality for searching for amphibians. All three species of newt, smooth, palmate and crested occur, together with the common toad and common frog. Being National Trust property, it is illegal to collect any natural specimens (including flowers) but this does not deter small boys from collecting frogspawn, tadpoles and newts, though to what extent they are responsible for the apparent decline of amphibians is always difficult to measure.

Grass snakes are abundant and often to be seen sunning themselves on the open plains where common lizards are also widespread. Slow worms, mainly in the more wooded areas, tend to hide away beneath logs and stones.

BOX HILL AND THE NORTH DOWNS

Certainly the best place in the vicinity of London for studying the natural history of chalk downland Box Hill is, in fact, one of the best examples of its kind in Britain. With thousands of visitors swarming over it each weekend it is surprising how well preserved the flora and fauna are. One of the traditional beauty spots sought out by Londoners, it has probably sparked off more budding young naturalists than any other area, for here one can hardly fail to find something unusual and interesting. For those wishing to make a detailed study of the area Juniper Hall Field Centre provides laboratory and other facilities for students. Courses are arranged at all levels and much of the study takes place in the field.

The first view of Box Hill coming south from London is usually from across the River Mole, and from this direction the vegetation, dominated by box trees *Buxus semporvirens* with their small dark green leaves, is evident. This tree is very local in its distribution, being found only on calcareous soils in southern England. Among the other trees which are noticeable from a distance are the whitebeam *Sorbus aria* with pale foliage, the yew *Taxus baccata* with almost black foliage, the white poplar *Populus alba*, the grey poplar *P. canescens* and the sycamore *Acer pseudoplatanus* var *purpureum* which has a purple colouration on the underside of the leaves.

Also on Box Hill magnificent beech woods of *Fagus sylvatica* are found. Tall, dark and cathedral-like, a beech wood in summer is one of the finest sights of the English countryside. Only the odd ray of sunlight manages to filter through the dense canopy of pale-green leaves, and the floor below seems almost devoid of vegetation. But even among the deep litter of golden-brown beech leaves one may discover a very interesting flora. Dog's mercury *Mercurialis perennis*, a plant often associated with badger setts (or more likely vice versa) is particularly abundant, as is the wood garlic *Allium ursinum*. Another characteristic find is one which probably has more names than any other English plant—*Arum maculatum*, known variously as the cuckoo-pint, parson-in-the-pulpit, lords-and-ladies and by many other local names. Some of the helleborines can sometimes be found. These rather inconspicuous orchids may often be overlooked but some of them are extremely beautiful; the most abundant is the broad helleborine *Epipactis helleborine*, which is a delicate purple colour. One of Britain's strangest orchids is also found beneath the beech trees; this is the saprophytic bird's-nest orchid, *Neottia nidus-avis*, which has no green, and produces a large spike of pale-brown flowers.

Box Hill is famous for its orchids, and although an experienced searcher will probably find a dozen or more species, it often seems remarkable that there are any left at all. How many of the Londoners trampling, picnicking, playing football and so forth, realise that in so doing they are probably crushing flowers such as the man orchid *Aceras anthropophorum* which takes several years to mature? Fortunately Box Hill, like Bookham Common, is owned by the National Trust and it is illegal to collect or pick wild flowers there. Most species of flora seem to be holding their own but in the case of orchids the balance is precarious and for this reason the names of the species and exact localities are not normally disclosed.

Among the characteristics of chalk downs are the grasslands, but over the last two decades these have been changed drastically by the advent of myxomatosis. This disease devastated the rabbit population, the result being that much of the chalk grassland, no longer grazed by the rabbits, was soon invaded by scrub. The plants characteristic of chalk grasslands include the pretty lavender-blue scabious *Scabiosa columbaria*, the bright yellow bird's-foot trefoil and many other most attractive English flowers. Much of the scrub on Box Hill is in patches on the grassland or along the edges of woods; the shrubs which characterise it are particularly attractive in autumn when laden with berries. The cornel or dogwood *Thelycrania sanguinea* and wayfaring tree *Viburnum lantana* have blackish berries; the hawthorn *Crataegus monogyna*, spindle *Euonymus europaeus*, roses *Rosa spp* and several others have red or orange berries. Old man's beard *Clematis vitalba*, with feathery beard-like fruits from which it takes its name, straggles over many of the bushes. Beneath them wild strawberries *Gragaria vesca* are to be found alongside the notorious deadly nightshade *Atropa belladonna*.

Equally interesting on Box Hill are the insects and other invertebrates. The famous box trees are the home of *Hyptiotes paradoxus*, an unusual spider known from only a few other places in Britain. The web built by this spider is unique—it is a triangular snare. The spider holds one corner taut then releases the slack silk web and when an insect touches the web enmeshes it. The whole procedure of building its web and catching its prey is incredibly complicated and requires considerable co-ordination of movement from the spider. Another very rare spider known mainly from Surrey and chiefly found on broad-leaved trees is *Dictyna viridissima*, which is a vivid green with markings of rust on the legs and body. This species has also been recorded as near to central London as Kingston, Wimbledon and Tooting. One of the most interesting spiders to be found on Box Hill is undoubtedly *Atypus affinis*, often incorrectly known as the trap-door spider. Its web is in fact quite different from those of the trap-doors and although classified in the sub-order Mygalomorphae, to which the trap-door spiders belong, it is placed in a distinct family, the *Atypidae*.

Box Hill is rich in *Orthoptera* (grasshoppers, bush crickets, etc) and 12 of the 35 or so British species have been recorded there in recent years. A further 5 species are known from older records.

On a sunny summer day Box Hill is a first-rate spot for the lepidopterist. The more abundant species of butterfly found on the grassy slopes of the chalk scarp and in the edges of the woodlands include ringlet, orange tip, speckled wood, green-hairstreak, dingy skipper, grizzled skipper, silver spotted skipper, wall brown, dark green fritillary, comma, common blue and chalk hill blue. Many other species have also been collected including some interesting variants and rare species.

Chalk downland is one of the finest habitats for molluscs and the fauna of Box Hill is rich in molluscan species. The so-called Roman or edible snail *Helix pomatia* is widespread on the North Downs, and though at one time believed to be an introduced alien (hence its name) it has been shown to be present in deposits which antedate the Roman occupation of Britain. An interesting species, probably quite widespread though rarely found by even the most ardent conchologist, as it frequently burrows, is the blind snail *Ceciloides acicula*. It is fairly abundant on Box Hill and can be found by examining the loose soil thrown up from rabbit burrows, or by digging in the loose soil around plant roots. Some miles north of Box Hill, still on the North Downs at White Hill, Chaldon, is one of the few localities in Britain where the top snail *Helicella elegans* occurs. Another rather local species *Pupilla muscorum* is also found on the North Downs; probably an introduced species, it is normally found in Mediterranean countries. In shape it resembles the attractive marine top shells, though it is less brightly coloured.

One of the few areas around London for which detailed studies of molluscs have been made is Devilsden Wood (TQ 3057) and the adjacent downs, near Coulsdon in Surrey. In a series of visits to a variety of habitats in the area C. P. Castell and A. W. Jones recorded forty-five species of slugs and snails. The greatest number and variety of species was recorded from the woodland and grassland on the chalk, the clay nearby was poor in molluscs. The Roman snail was found mainly along the edge of the wood, in hedges and scrubby areas, and the moss snail *Pupilla muscorum*, a rather local species, was fairly abundant in the downland turf. Other species likely to be encountered on the chalk included the round-mouthed snail *Pomatias elegans*, the slippery snail *Cochlicopa lubrica*, the ribbed snail *Vallonia costata*, the strawberry snail *Hygromia striolata*, the Kentish snail *Monacha cantiana*, the glossy snail *Oxychilus helveticus* and the pellucid snail *Vitrina pellucida*.

Along the downs from Box Hill, Betchworth, Colley Hill to Reigate Hill there are numerous exposures of the Middle and

Lower Chalk on the steep south-facing scarp of the downs. These exposures have produced many fine specimens of fossils, particularly brachiopods, echinoids and ammonites. In nearly all cases a hammer and chisel is necessary to collect and, of course, permission from the landowner.

HAREFIELD GREAT PIT

This disused chalk pit at Harefield, north-west Middlesex (TQ 0490), is now used as a rubbish dump; the depth of the rubbish is about 180 feet and almost level with the top of the chalk exposure. Permission to visit must be obtained from the owners, W. W. Drinkwater (Willesden) Ltd, Dudden Hill Lane, Willesden, London NW 10 and, as the site is classified as a Site of Special Scientific Interest, permission must also be obtained from the GLC Parks Department.

The top of the chalk exposure is the Coranguinum Zone, and the top foot or so has been bored by the burrows of callianassid crustaceans, which were originally described in 1923 as a new species of worm under the name *Terebella harefieldensis*.

It is interesting to compare the succession at Harefield Pit with that at Charlton (page 57). The continued transgression of the Lower Eocene Beds over the eroded chalk surface can be seen: at Charlton the earlier Thanet Sands rest on the chalk with the top of the sands burrowed whereas at Harefield, which is further inland and later in geological time, it is the top of the chalk which is burrowed.

At Harefield the chalk is overlaid with the basal Pebble Bed of the Reading Beds. Above the Pebble Beds are the sands and loams of the Reading Beds themselves, in which can be found impressions of leaves. Above the Reading Beds is the so-called London Clay Basement Bed, which contains a hard limestone band and nodules containing molluscs. The limestone is bored by the marine bivalve *Martesia saxorum* and there are remains of the coral *Paracyathus crassus* on top of the limestone, indicating a stable environment. Above this bed is about five foot of clayey sands with molluscs and a few sharks' teeth. Above this is the true London Clay, which is not exposed, and the top of the hill is capped with gravels.

EPPING FOREST

Lying to the north-east of London, in the county of Essex, Epping Forest is one of the favourite recreation grounds of Londoners. Each weekend, when the weather is fine, hundreds of the city dwellers descend on the peace and quiet of the forest for a few hours 'away from it all'. Obviously this has an adverse effect on the wildlife, but fortunately the average picknickers do not wander far and large areas of the forest remain relatively undisturbed.

Originally Epping Forest was part of a vast hunting preserve known as Waltham Forest, which belonged to Waltham Abbey. During the Reformation the lands of Waltham Abbey reverted to the crown, were subsequently divided and eventually passed into private hands. By the eighteenth century the maintenance of the royal hunting rights had ceased, and there was a strong pressure to enclose the land and bring it under cultivation. In the mid-nineteenth century nearby Hainault Forest was almost completely destroyed in as short a time as six weeks. Similar threats to Epping Forest were only staved off with long and expensive lawsuits, some 6,000 acres eventually being acquired by the City of London Corporation for the use of the public.

Most of Epping Forest is on London Clay, but there are many areas of sand, boulder clay and gravels, notably around High Beach. The boulder clay, particularly noticeable and widespread in Essex, is evidence of the extent of glaciation during the Pleistocene Period. At the time of the glaciation, when the various soils were deposited, England was connected to the continent of Europe and southern England was dominated by bare windswept tundra and permafrost which extended as far south as central France. In the gravels of High Beach many worked flints and flakes and a few tranchet axes have been found, and dated as being from the Mesolithic Period.

The extensive woodlands are mainly of fairly recent date; in the eighteenth century they were very widely felled for timber. The trees which dominate the forest are oak, beech, hornbeam and birch; in many places the beech, and hornbeam in particular, have been extensively pollarded. This, although mutilating the trees, does provide an interesting habitat—birds such as redstarts are attracted to the pollarded hornbeams. The flora is richer and more varied than might be expected from a habitat mostly on the heavy London Clay, but it is perhaps for the fungi that Epping Forest is particularly well known. The London Natural History Society, Essex Field Club and other natural history societies hold 'fungus forays' in the forest and over 800 species have been recorded, including such rarities as earthstars *Geaster bryantii*.

Another group of plants well worth examining in Epping Forest is the fern. R. M. Payne, writing in 1959, was able to note that 'the persistence of the fern flora of the forest is in pleasant contrast to the melancholy loss or diminution of many of its flowering plants'. Although only one species is thought to have been exterminated in the twentieth century—the soft prickly shield fern *Polystichum setiferum*—only three species are widespread and common. They are bracken *Pteridium aquilinum*, broad buckler *Dryopteris dilatata* and the male fern *Dryopteris filix-mas*. The lady fern *Athyrium filix-femina*, the mountain buckler fern *Thelypteris oreopteris* and adder's tongue *Ophioglossum vulgatum*, are found mainly in the northern parts of the forest. Altogether some sixteen or seventeen species of fern are likely to be encountered, though some are very rare and restricted to a few isolated colonies.

Although park deer can be seen in many of the London parks, Epping Forest is one of the nearest places to central London with a thriving herd of wild deer. The fallow deer found in the forest are slightly unusual in that most of them are dark and lack the usual conspicuous dappled pattern. The herd has been somewhat depleted in recent years and now probably numbers no more than a hundred individuals. It is thought that the high number of road casualties which occur along the main roads passing through the forest, particularly the A11, may have been an important factor in reducing the numbers. The deer are most frequently seen in the northern part of the forest. Formerly red deer lived in Epping but they were removed during the early part of the nineteenth century. Roe deer were introduced in the 1880s but although they flourished for a number of years they had died out by the early 1920s. With the spread of muntjac deer in nearby areas it seems likely that these animals will colonise Epping Forest within the next decade.

With regard to other types of fauna, badgers and foxes are locally abundant, stoats and weasels are occasionally seen. Rabbits are widespread and hares are locally abundant, particularly in the northern parts of the forest. Until recently red squirrels existed in small numbers, but it is extremely doubtful that any still survive. Various species of shrews, mice, voles and bats commonly occur, but there are far too few records to suggest which of these is the most numerous.

In recent years, members of the Essex Field Club have been extremely active in recording the reptiles and amphibians found in the forest. Adders have been found to be numerous in places, but are very often persecuted by visitors; the grass snake is still common in most parts of the forest; the slow worm is widespread and probably fairly common, though rarely seen; the common lizard is abundant in most of the plains and open spaces. The amphibians have suffered in recent years from the attention of small boys—in particular the common frog, a species once common but now rather scarce, probably because its spawn is usually laid in shallow water near the edge of the pond. The common toad, on the other hand, is still quite abundant and breeds in many of the ponds; its spawn is wrapped round pondweed in deeper waters. Of the newts, the palmate is the most numerous; the smooth newt, though equally widespread, occurs in smaller numbers. The crested newt is only occasionally found though it may be more abundant than the records suggest as it prefers deeper water where it is less easily seen.

The numerous ponds are perhaps one of the most interesting, though possibly one of the most vulnerable, of all the habitats within the forest. They contain a rich and varied flora and fauna which is unfortunately extremely susceptible to the pressures of visitors. Apart from the depletions of small boys, untidy Londoners dump refuse such as oil cans in them, often causing extensive pollution. Baldwin's Pond is one of the largest, though it has regrettably been suffering from disturbance in recent years. In his book *Field Natural History* Alfred Leutcher discusses the flora and fauna of the pond in some detail (in fact many of the examples throughout the book are drawn from Epping Forest). The fish recorded were crucian and common carp, rudd, eel, perch, three-spined stickleback and pike. Palmate, crested and smooth newts were recorded as well as both common frog and toad. Of the many species of freshwater molluscs, the most interesting were probably the freshwater mussels: the painter's mussel *Unio pictorum*, swan mussel *Anodonta cygnea* and duck mussel *A. anatina* were all noted. The water spiders *Argyroneta aquatica*, *Pirata piscatorius* and *Dolomedes fimbriatus* were seen together with a wealth of other interesting invertebrates.

As would be expected in an area of the size of Epping Forest the avifauna also is rich. Tree pipits breed in many places and, until its recent catastrophic decline, the red-backed shrike bred in small numbers in many parts. It remains to be seen whether they manage to regain their former status. Perhaps the most famous birds of Epping Forest are the redstarts which, as already mentioned, favour the pollarded hornbeams, where the shy and elusive hawfinch may also be seen occasionally. Epping Forest is one of the nearest localities to central London where nightingales may be heard and seen, a few pairs breeding in the more inaccessible parts of the forest each year. The tree pipit breeds throughout the area and is usually to be found in the more open woodland, normally on the clearings.

The lists of the fauna and flora are extensive and for greater detail the reader is referred to reports of the Essex Field Club, who regularly publish papers on the forest. Articles on the forest also appear in the *London Naturalist*.

London's birds

THIS LIST OMITS all extreme rarities and vagrants. For up-to-date information on every bird recorded within twenty miles of London, the reader is referred to the *London Bird Report*, published annually by the London Natural History Society.

The list follows the British Ornithologists' Union's *The Status of the Birds of Great Britain and Ireland* (1971). The term 'throughout London' should always be qualified by 'where suitable habitat is available'.

RED-THROATED DIVER *Gavia stellata*
An occasional winter and passage visitor on open waters such as the reservoirs and larger gravel pits. Great northern divers and black-throated divers are also occasionally seen on the reservoirs, but the red-throated occurs most frequently
LITTLE GREBE *Podiceps ruficollis*
Present all the year and often breeds on gravel pits and similar waters. In late autumn and winter they sometimes gather into flocks
BLACK-NECKED GREBE *P. nigricollis*
An occasional visitor in all months of the year. Most numerous in late summer and autumn particularly on reservoirs
SLAVONIAN GREBE *P. auritus*
A rare winter visitor to reservoirs and other larger open waters. Has occasionally been observed in the central parks
RED-NECKED GREBE *P. griseigena*
A rare visitor to reservoirs and other waters
GREAT-CRESTED GREBE *P. cristatus*
Present all year. It breeds on many of the larger waters in and around London. During the autumn months large numbers are often seen on reservoirs, lakes and gravel pits
CORMORANT *Phalacrocorax carbo*
A regular visitor to the reservoirs. Also occasionally recorded in Regent's Park, Hyde Park and St James's Park—though in St James's Park there are also pinioned birds
HERON *Ardea cinerea*
Resident. Occasionally visits central London parks, and is sometimes seen flying over. Recently they have nested in Regent's and Battersea Parks. Notable heronries are at Walthamstow reservoirs and in Kempton Park

MUTE SWAN   *Cygnus olor*
Found throughout London and breeds on many waters. Particularly abundant
on the Thames, where each July the picturesque swan-upping ceremony takes
place when representatives of the liveried companies and the crown mark the
swans. Wild swans (whooper or Bewick's) are occasionally seen flying over
London

GEESE   *Anser* sp
Flocks of migrating geese are seen almost annually. Whitefronted geese (*A.
albifrons*) are the most frequently identified. Many of the single birds recorded
are escapes

CANADA GOOSE   *Branta canadensis*
An introduced species now firmly established. Breeds in many parks, gravel
pits, etc. There are some 200 birds on the Serpentine in Hyde Park and Kensington Gardens. Some of these birds can be seen flying between Hyde Park,
St James's Park and the grounds of Buckingham Palace

SHELDUCK   *Tadorna tadorna*
An annual visitor, but only in small numbers over most of London. Large
numbers recorded on the Thames downstream from Woolwich

MANDARIN DUCK   *Aix galericulata*
An introduced species which is now well established on the south-western outskirts of London, particularly along the River Mole

WIGEON   *Anas penelope*
A winter visitor to most open waters. The largest flocks are usually recorded
from Staines reservoir

GADWALL   *A. strepera*
Breeds in small numbers around London and is seen on many of the reservoirs
and gravel pits

TEAL   *A. crecca*
Mainly a winter visitor to the reservoirs, gravel pits, marshes, etc. It is one of
the most numerous species of duck around London but rarely seen in central
London except during severe weather

MALLARD   *A. platyrhynchos*
A common and widespread species, occurring throughout London at all times
of the year. Even breeds in the centre of the metropolis. Large flocks are seen
annually on the reservoirs and, more recently, on the Thames and adjacent
marshes

PINTAIL   *A. acuta*
Mainly a winter visitor, though rarely in large numbers. The largest flocks are
recorded from the Thames and adjacent marshes around Dartford

GARGANEY   *A. querquedula*
A scarce passage migrant

SHOVELER   *A. clypeata*
Mainly a winter visitor, though a few breed on some reservoirs and gravel pits

POCHARD *Aythya ferina*
Present all year, breeding throughout London. Often occurs with tufted duck, in summer and winter, but usually in smaller numbers. The largest flocks in recent years have been recorded on the Thames around Woolwich

FERRUGINOUS DUCK *A. nyroca*
An irregular visitor. Has been recorded from Hyde Park

TUFTED DUCK *A. fuligula*
Present all the year and breeds throughout London. It is also a common winter visitor. Some of the largest winter counts for this species are from Barn Elms reservoir

SCAUP *A. marila*
An infrequent visitor to open waters throughout London

LONG-TAILED DUCK *Clangula hyemalis*
A very scarce winter visitor to the reservoirs

COMMON SCOTER *Melanitta nigra*
A scarce passage migrant, usually seen on the reservoirs in spring or mid-summer. The velvet scoter is also occasionally recorded

GOLDENEYE *Bucephala clangula*
A scarce winter visitor mainly occurring on the reservoirs

SMEW *Mergus albellus*
The London reservoirs are renowned as one of the best places to see the smew. It is a winter visitor reaching maximum numbers during January and February, particularly during hard weather. Stoke Newington, Staines and Brent reservoirs are all good localities

RED-BREASTED MERGANSER *M. serrator*
A winter visitor occurring in small numbers, mainly on the reservoirs

GOOSANDER *M. merganser*
A winter visitor to the reservoirs; maximum numbers are usually recorded from Staines reservoir

SPARROWHAWK *Accipiter nisus*
At one time a widespread species, even breeding in the suburbs. Now mainly recorded from well-wooded areas on the outskirts of London

KESTREL *Falco tinnunculus*
A common breeding bird, breeding throughout London including the heart of the metropolis

MERLIN *F. columbarius*
A scarce visitor, only a few individuals being recorded each year

HOBBY *F. subbuteo*
Summer visitor breeding in a few localities on the outskirts of London, details of which are supressed to protect the birds

RED-LEGGED PARTRIDGE *Alectoris rufa*
A well-established introduced species which breeds on many of the larger commons and on farmland surrounding London

PARTRIDGE *Perdix perdix*
A similar distribution to the red-legged partridge but possibly more common in Middlesex and Surrey

QUAIL *Coturnix coturnix*
A scarce summer visitor which probably breeds on the outskirts of London in the Darenth Valley, Kent, and a few other localities

PHEASANT *Phasianus colchicus*
A well-established alien. Common in wooded areas in outer suburbs

WATER RAIL *Rallus aquaticus*
Widespread in suitable habitats in London and recorded every month of the year but a difficult species to observe. May breed at several localities

MOORHEN *Gallinula chloropus*
A widespread breeding species, common on waters throughout London

COOT *Fulica atra*
A common breeding species and winter visitor. Breeds throughout London, including the central parks. Large flocks occur in winter on the reservoirs and gravel pits, etc

OYSTERCATCHER *Haematopus ostralegus*
An annual passage migrant in very small numbers

LAPWING *Vanellus vanellus*
Breeds on farmland, marshes and sewage farms surrounding London. In winter, particularly during hard weather, often occurs in parks and on playing fields in large numbers

GOLDEN PLOVER *Charadrius apricarius*
A winter visitor occurring in small numbers at many places on the outskirts of London. The largest flocks are normally around Staines Moor and Heathrow Airport

RINGED PLOVER *C. hiaticula*
A scarce passage migrant to many gravel pits and sewage farms, etc. Also breeds at a few localities near London, such as Nazeing, Stanwellmoor, Rainham Marsh and Thamesmead

LITTLE RINGED PLOVER *C. dubius*
A regular breeding species since 1944. Although some 40 pairs nest in gravel pits around London each year the localities are supressed as it is one of Britain's rarest breeding birds

WHIMBREL *Numenius phaeopus*
A passage migrant, occurring in small numbers

CURLEW *N. arquata*
A regular passage migrant and scarce winter visitor to sewage farms, reservoirs, the Thames marshes, etc

BLACK-TAILED GODWIT *Limosa limosa*
A scarce passage migrant. The bar-tailed godwit is also recorded occasionally

Page 125 (*above*) Several of the parks in and around London contain herds of deer. These are fallow deer in Richmond Park; (*below*) the black rat is a species which has become rare in Britain, one of its few strongholds being in London

Page 126 (above) The stoat is still fairly widespread around London, though it appears to be less abundant in Middlesex; (below) the noctule bat is one of the largest British bats. It rarely comes into the roofs of houses, but can often be seen hunting for crickets over rubbish tips

SPOTTED REDSHANK *Tringa erythropus*
A passage migrant, occurring in small numbers

REDSHANK *T. totanus*
Present all the year. Breeds in a few localities on the outskirts of London, such as Rye Meads sewage farm and the Thames marshes. Large flocks (up to 150) winter on the latter

GREENSHANK *T. nebularia*
A fairly common passage migrant

GREEN SANDPIPER *T. ochropus*
A passage migrant and winter visitor to marshes and sewage farms

WOOD SANDPIPER *T. glareola*
A passage migrant, usually seen at sewage farms, etc

COMMON SANDPIPER *T. hypoleucos*
Mainly a passage migrant. Most abundant along the Thames, on the reservoirs and some sewage farms

SNIPE *Gallinago gallinago*
Mainly a winter visitor to marshes and sewage farms where it sometimes breeds in small numbers. During cold weather the numbers on sewage farms often build up to astronomic figures

WOODCOCK *Scolopax rusticola*
Breeds in small numbers on the outskirts of London, particularly in Surrey. May breed as far in as Richmond Park

JACK SNIPE *Lymnocryptes minimus*
A winter visitor, mainly to sewage farms. Only rarely (usually in severe weather) do numbers reach double figures

LITTLE STINT *Calidris minuta*
A scarce passage migrant and winter visitor to reservoirs, sewage farms and marshes

DUNLIN *C. alpina*
Mainly a winter visitor, particularly abundant on the Thames marshes where about 1,500 may be present in mid-winter

CURLEW SANDPIPER *C. testacea*
A fairly regular visitor in autumn to Perry Oaks sewage farm and Rainham Marsh. Elsewhere very scarce

RUFF *Philomachus pugnax*
Mainly passage migrant but winters at Perry Oaks sewage farm on the Thames marshes and a few other localities

COMMON GULL *Larus canus*
An abundant visitor, mainly in winter

HERRING GULL *L. argentatus*
Abundant and widespread, particularly in winter. For the last few years pairs have nested in Regent's Park and St James's Park

H

LESSER BLACK-BACKED GULL *L. fuscus*
Abundant and widespread, particularly in winter. A pair has recently attempted to breed in Regent's Park

GREAT BLACK-BACKED GULL *L. marinus*
Mainly an autumn migrant and winter visitor particularly abundant on reservoirs and playing fields

BLACK-HEADED GULL *L. ridibundus*
Formerly bred at Perry Oaks sewage farm. Common and often very tame winter visitor. Feeds from the hand in many parks in central London

LITTLE GULL *L. minutus*
Occurs annually in small numbers, particularly at Staines reservoir

KITTIWAKE *Rissa tridactyla*
A scarce visitor, mainly to reservoirs

BLACK TERN *Chlidonias niger*
A regular passage migrant, particularly abundant at Staines reservoir

COMMON TERN *Sterna hirundo*
On the reservoirs, a common passage migrant—though usually indistinguishable from Arctic tern. Occasionally breeds at a few localities near to London such as King George VI reservoir and Broxbourne gravel pit

LITTLE TERN *S. albifrons*
An occasional passage migrant. The roseate tern is also recorded in most years

SANDWICH TERN *S. sandvicensis*
A scarce passage migrant, most likely to be encountered on Staines reservoir

ROCK DOVE (Feral pigeon) *Columba livia*
Widespread, but as a breeding species largely restricted to the heavily urbanised areas

STOCK DOVE *C. oenas*
A widespread breeding species which is seen even in central London parks

WOOD PIGEON *C. palumbus*
A common breeding species which has even adapted to nesting in central London

TURTLE DOVE *Streptopelia turtur*
A fairly common summer migrant breeding in most of the larger woods and parks surrounding the London suburbs

COLLARED DOVE *S. decaocto*
This species colonised Britain relatively recently from SE Europe. On the continent and in other parts of Britain it is often seen in towns, but around London it is restricted mainly to the suburbs. It is particularly abundant in Surrey

CUCKOO *Cuculus canorus*
A summer visitor breeding in rural areas, large parks and woods. Occasionally seen on passage in more built-up areas

BARN OWL *Tyto alba*
Breeds in the outer suburbs and rural areas but is nowhere common

LITTLE OWL *Athene noctua*
A well-established introduced species. Breeds in scattered localities throughout the outer suburbs. Commonest in Surrey, but possibly decreasing

TAWNY OWL *Strix aluco*
The most common and widespread owl in London. Breeds in some central London parks and is widespread in the suburbs

SHORT-EARED OWL *Asio flammeus*
An erratic winter visitor. In some years appears in large numbers, depending on the birds' breeding success and the size of the vole population on which it preys. Unsually seen on marshes, commons and sewage farms

NIGHTJAR *Caprimulgus europaeus*
A summer visitor which breeds in small numbers on the heaths and commons around London such as Ongar Park, Essex; Oxshott, Headley and Walton Heaths, Surrey

SWIFT *Apus apus*
A widespread summer visitor. Breeds in the older suburbs as far into London as Kensington. Gathers in large numbers over reservoirs and sewage farms to feed

KINGFISHER *Alcedo atthis*
Breeds along many of the rivers in the green belt. Occasionally seen over suburban lakes and ponds

WRYNECK *Jynx torquilla*
A summer visitor which was at one time a fairly widespread breeding bird in Britain with some 20 or more pairs nesting close to London; now the wryneck only breeds in two or three of its old haunts

GREEN WOODPECKER *Picus viridis*
A widespread species breeding in parks in the outer suburbs and rural areas. Occasionally seen in the more built-up areas

GREAT SPOTTED WOODPECKER *Dendrocopus major*
Commoner than the previous species. A frequent visitor to suburban bird-tables. May occasionally attempt to breed in some of the central parks, as they have sometimes been seen

LESSER SPOTTED WOODPECKER *D. minor*
Breeds in many woodlands and may be the commonest species of woodpecker in some areas, notably Surrey

WOODLARK *Lullula arborea*
Shortly after the war, woodlarks were first recorded as breeding in the London area and the population started to increase around London after an almost total absence. By the 1950s they were breeding in many places close to London including Richmond Park, Wimbledon Common and Putney Heath. Since then the population has again declined and it is doubtful whether any woodlarks still breed in London's immediate vicinity

SKYLARK *Alauda arvensis*
Breeds on most commons and suitable open ground in and around London

SAND MARTIN *Riparia riparia*
A locally abundant summer visitor. Breeds colonially wherever suitable habitat is available. Occasionally colonies are found in drainpipes; these have been noted near Wimbledon and at Barking

SWALLOW *Hirundo rustica*
A common summer visitor breeding mainly in the outer suburbs, though a pair have nested in Regent's Park

HOUSE MARTIN *Delichon urbica*
An abundant summer visitor which nests well into the suburbs. The nearest colonies to central London are probably those in the Fulham and Primrose Hill areas

YELLOW WAGTAIL *Motacilla flava*
A summer migrant mainly restricted to marshes and sewage farms on the outskirts of London. Has been known to nest well in towards central London, as far as Vauxhall Bridge! The continental blue-headed race is occasionally seen

GREY WAGTAIL *M. cinerea*
Breeds in only a few localities, mainly on the outskirts of London, such as at Beddington sewage farm, Surrey; Brent reservoir, Middlesex; and Ruxley gravel pit, Kent

PIED WAGTAIL *M. alba*
Breeds in small numbers throughout the suburbs. In recent years has also nested in Bloomsbury, Brunswick Square and the Cripplegate area. Often gathers in large flocks to roost—one notable roost is at Hammersmith Broadway. The continental race known as the white wagtail is sometimes encountered

TREE PIPIT *Anthus trivialis*
Breeds at scattered localities throughout the outer suburbs and surrounding countryside such as Epping Forest and Ongar Park Wood, Essex; Mill Hill and Potters Bar, Middlesex; Westerham, Kent; Richmond Park and Wimbledon Common, Surrey

MEADOW PIPIT *A. pratensis*
Breeds in small numbers in outer suburbs and in areas around London and occurs on passage in most London parks, etc. During the winter often gathers in flocks

ROCK PIPIT *A. spinoletta*
Mainly a winter visitor, in small numbers, to reservoirs, sewage farms, etc. Also along the Thames foreshore. (The water pipit, a race of the rock pipit, is also encountered in these areas)

RED-BACKED SHRIKE *Lanius collurio*
A summer visitor which just over a decade ago was a fairly widespread breeding bird in the countryside around London and even on one or two of the larger suburban heaths and commons. The population is so reduced that no information is available concerning the remaining one or two pairs

GREAT GREY SHRIKE *L. excubitor*
An erratic visitor to commons and heaths in the suburbs, usually in winter

WAXWING   *Bombycilla garrulus*
An irruptive species which is occasionally seen in the London suburbs in winter
WREN   *Troglodytes troglodytes*
Breeds throughout London. Found in several central London parks and has nested on the bombed sites, etc
HEDGE SPARROW   *Prunella modularis*
A widespread and abundant resident breeding species in all but the most densely built-up areas
ROBIN   *Erithacus rubecula*
A common and widespread breeding species. It breeds in most suburban areas and several central parks and squares
NIGHTINGALE   *Luscinia megarhynchos*
A summer visitor which breeds in wooded open spaces around London such as Epping Forest, Essex; Dartford Heath, Kent and Bookham Common, Surrey
BLACK REDSTART   *Phoenicurus ochrurus*
A London speciality. At one time famous as a colonist of the bombed sites in the Cripplegate area of the City of London, most recent breeding records are from power stations and similar sites. Littlebrook power station, Kent, and Croydon power station, Surrey, are regular nesting sites
REDSTART   *P. phoenicurus*
A summer visitor which breeds in a few well-wooded areas on the outskirts of London, such as Epping Forest and Richmond Park
WHINCHAT   *Saxicola rubetra*
A fairly common passage migrant and summer visitor which also breeds at a few localities, mainly in Kent and Essex
STONECHAT   *S. torquata*
A few pairs breed in the open countryside around London, and the odd bird is seen in the suburban parks, commons, sewage farms, etc, mainly during the winter months
WHEATEAR   *Oenanthe oenanthe*
A passage migrant which is usually seen on open heaths, commons, golf courses, playing fields, etc
RING OUZEL   *Turdus torquatus*
A scarce passage migrant
BLACKBIRD   *T. merula*
Widespread throughout London, even in some built-up areas. Often nests in bizarre situations, such as under the bonnet of a car
FIELDFARE   *T. pilaris*
A winter visitor which can be seen feeding in large numbers on open fields, many parks, golf courses, playing fields, etc
REDWING   *T. musicus*
A common winter visitor often seen feeding on open fields, in company with fieldfares, etc

SONG THRUSH *T. ericetorum*

A widespread breeding species which nests throughout suburbs and also in many of central parks and squares. Many migrants are also present during the winter

MISTLE THRUSH *T. viscivorus*

Widespread throughout London. Breeds in most suburban parks and some of the central parks and squares

GRASSHOPPER WARBLER *Locustella naevia*

A summer migrant which breeds in the countryside surrounding London such as Rye Meads in Herts; Ashstead Common, Bookham Common, Epsom Common and Prince's Coverts in Surrey

SEDGE WARBLER *Acrocephalus schoenobaenus*

A summer migrant breeding in most suitable habitats in the area surrounding London, the nearest breeding locality being at the Brent reservoir

REED WARBLER *A. scirpaceus*

A summer visitor which breeds in most suitable habitats in the countryside surrounding London, the nearest being at Brent reservoir, Barn Elms reservoir and Richmond Park

GARDEN WARBLER *Sylvia borin*

A summer visitor. Less widespread than the previous species, found mainly in outer suburbs and beyond. The most central nesting areas are probably Hampstead, Dulwich and Richmond

BLACKCAP *S. atricapilla*

A widespread summer migrant in London and surrounding countryside. Breeds in most woods and parks and even large gardens. A few pairs nest each year in Holland Park, Kensington Gardens and Regent's Park

WHITETHROAT *S. communis*

A summer migrant which suffered a severe decline recently but is slowly recovering

LESSER WHITETHROAT *S. curruca*

A summer migrant; breeds at many localities in the countryside surrounding London, but distribution is always patchy. Seen on migration in many London parks

WILLOW WARBLER *Phylloscopus trochilus*

A widespread summer visitor breeding in wooded parks and commons in the suburbs. Has recently bred in Kensington Gardens

CHIFFCHAFF *P. collybita*

Mainly a summer visitor sharing a similar distribution to the willow warbler. A few individuals winter each year

GOLDCREST *Regulus regulus*

Breeds in scattered localities around London such as Epping Forest, Essex; Bushy Park and Hampstead, Middlesex; and Kew Gardens, Surrey. The similar and closely related firecrest is occasionally observed

PIED FLYCATCHER   *Muscicapa hypoleuca*
A regular passage migrant
SPOTTED FLYCATCHER   *M. striata*
Breeds throughout the suburbs in parks, large gardens, etc. In recent years up
to thirty pairs have attempted to breed in Hyde Park and Kensington Gardens
LONG-TAILED TIT   *Aegithalos caudatus*
Breeds in the outer suburban areas, mainly on overgrown commons, woods,
etc. During cold weather often moves through the suburbs in noisy flocks
MARSH TIT   *Parus palustris*
Breeds in woods and parks, mainly in the outer suburbs
WILLOW TIT   *P. atricapillus*
Breeds at scattered localities on the outskirts of London such as Epping Forest
in Essex or Selsdon and Banstead Woods in Surrey
COAL TIT   *P. ater*
Found in many of the suburbs of London and surrounding countryside but
nowhere as abundant as the two previous species. Breeds in Regent's Park,
Hyde Park, Kensington Gardens, etc
GREAT TIT   *P. major*
A widespread species breeding throughout London
BLUE TIT   *P. caeruleus*
A widespread species breeding throughout London. Tends to be more numerous
than the great tit
NUTHATCH   *Sitta europaea*
Breeds in most well-wooded suburban parks and woods. A visitor to bird tables
TREE CREEPER   *Certhia familiaris*
Breeds in some of the suburban woods such as Dulwich and possibly Holland
Park
CORN BUNTING   *Emberiza calandra*
A scarce breeding species in the outer suburbs and surrounding countryside
YELLOWHAMMER   *E. citrinella*
Mainly restricted to the outer suburbs as a breeding species. In winter some-
times gathers into large flocks
CIRL BUNTING   *E. cirlus*
A very local species breeding at one or two localities on the outskirts of London
REED BUNTING   *E. schoeniclus*
Breeds on rough pasturage, marshes and waste ground throughout outer
suburban areas. It is widespread in parks and commons in winter
CHAFFINCH   *Fringilla coelebs*
A resident species which breeds throughout the suburbs and in some central
parks
BRAMBLING   *F. montifringilla*
A winter visitor which is occasionally seen in most London parks and is fairly
abundant on agricultural land, sewage farms and marshes in the outer suburbs

GREENFINCH   *Chloris chloris*
A resident species which breeds throughout suburbs and in some central parks
GOLDFINCH   *Carduelis carduelis*
A resident species which breeds at scattered localities throughout the suburbs. Occasionally large roosting flocks are seen in roadside trees, even in the built-up areas
SISKIN   *C. spinus*
Mainly a winter visitor often seen in flocks in suburban gardens and in parks
REDPOLL   *C. flammea*
Breeds in small numbers as near to London as Wimbledon Common and Hampstead Heath. Larger flocks are often seen in winter
LINNET   *C. cannabina*
A widespread breeding species found mainly in rural areas but also breeding in a few suburban parks and large gardens
CROSSBILL   *Loxia curvirostra*
An irruptive species occasionally seen in London. A few pairs also nest in Kent and Surrey
BULLFINCH   *Pyrrhula pyrrhula*
Breeds throughout suburbs and in some of the central parks
HAWFINCH   *Coccothraustes coccothraustes*
A shy retiring bird which may, in fact, be more widespread than normally believed. Is well distributed in the outer suburban parks and gardens
HOUSE SPARROW   *Passer domesticus*
Ubiquitous, even in the heart of the built-up area
TREE SPARROW   *P. montanus*
A locally abundant breeding species almost entirely confined to commons, sewage farms, etc, in the outer suburbs and rural areas
STARLING   *Sturnus vulgaris*
One of the most successful of London's birds. A widespread breeding species. The large urban roost centred on Trafalgar Square and Whitehall is famous
JAY   *Garrulus glandarius*
A common breeding bird found in most suburban areas and many central London parks and squares
MAGPIE   *Pica pica*
From being a very rare bird at the turn of the century the magpie has spread throughout London and is often seen along railway lines and in the more over-grown parts of parks and commons
NUTCRACKER   *Nucifraga caryocatactes*
An irregular winter visitor to Britain. Occasionally it 'irrupts' from Scandi-navia, when it may turn up almost anywhere. The birds seen in Britain are the slender-billed form
JACKDAW   *Corvus monedula*
A locally common breeding species. The colony in Kensington Gardens has

hovered on the verge of extinction for several years but a few birds are still present

ROOK   *C. frugilegus*

Breeds in the rural areas around London, but in general is decreasing

CARRION CROW   *C. corone*

A common breeding species throughout the suburbs and even in the central London parks and squares. Often gathers in large flocks. Occasionally the hooded crow is also seen

Flora of central London

THIS LIST, BASED mainly on the records published by the London Natural History Society, is intended as a guide to the more widespread and abundant plants in central London. Most rarities and vagrants are excluded.

COMMON HORSETAIL *Equisetum arvense*
Several localities in central London
BRACKEN *Pteridium aquilinum*
Common on buildings, railway embankments and other shady places in London
MALE FERN *Dryopteris filix-mas*
Common. Fully grown plants are rather rare; known from several of the central parks
YEW *Taxus baccata*
Planted occasionally in parks, squares and churchyards
BUTTERCUPS *Ranunculus* sp
Two species are fairly common, notably *R. acris*, *R. repens* whilst three others are rare: *R. bulbosus*, *R. sceleratus* and *R. ficaria*. Kensington Gardens and Hyde Park are good localities for most of these
COMMON POPPY *Papaver rhoeas*
A fairly widespread species. Occurs alongside paths
OPIUM POPPY *P. somniferum*
A garden escape which occurs on waste-ground, and in parks occasionally
WALL ROCKET *Diplotaxis muralis*
Occurs in many parts of London, mainly along railway embankments
SHEPHERDS PURSE *Capsella bursa-pastoris*
Very common on most open spaces throughout London
HORSE RADISH *Armoracia rusticana*
A common garden escape found on waste ground, railway embankments, etc
LONDON ROCKET *Sisymbrium irio*
Now rare, but formerly abundant. Known from Tower of London area
WHITE CAMPION *Silene alba*
Locally abundant. Found in Chelsea, Paddington and several of the central parks. The bladder campion *S. vulgaris* is also found at some of the localities from which the white species is known

COMMON MOUSE-EAR CHICKWEED   *Cerastium holosteoides*
Abundant on waste ground
CHICKWEED   *Stellaria media*
Very common
PROCUMBENT PEARLWORT   *Sagina procumbens*
Widespread. Occurring mainly in stony areas such as paved paths, rockeries and around walls
PERFOLIATE CLAYTONIA   *Montia perfoliata*
A fairly widespread weed of gardens and parks in the Kensington and Chelsea area
MANY-SEEDED GOOSEFOOT   *Chenopodium polyspermum*
Common, even in central parks where it is a weed of flower beds
WHITE GOOSEFOOT   *C. album*
Very common
FIG-LEAVED GOOSEFOOT   *C. ficifolium*
Less common than the two previous species but occurs in several parks including Kensington Gardens, Primrose Hill and Battersea Park. The nettle-leaved goosefoot *C. murale* occurs, but only in a few localities mainly in the Kensington/Chelsea area
HASTATE ORACHE   *Altriplex hastata*
Common
COMMON MALLOW   *Malva sylvestris*
Common
DWARF MALLOW   *M. neglecta*
Fairly widespread; recorded from the central parks
CRANESBILLS   *Geranium* sp
Several of these have been recorded from Regent's Park, including *G. pratense*, *G. sanguineum*, *G. macrorrhizum* and *G. molle*. Other species have been recorded elsewhere in small numbers
SMALL BALSAM   *Impatiens parviflora*
A garden escape which has colonised several areas, notably Regent's Park and the railway embankments nearby
HIMALAYAN OR INDIAN BALSAM   *I. glandulifera*
A garden escape widespread in several parts of north London, notably alongside the Regent's Canal
TREE OF HEAVEN   *Ailanthus altissima*
A Chinese tree often planted in squares and gardens. Occurs as an escape throughout central London
SYCAMORE   *Acer pseudoplatanus*
A common tree even in central London
HORSE CHESTNUT   *Aesculus hippocastanum*
Originally from the Balkans now common throughout London, including central parks and squares

HOLLY *Ilex aquifolium*
Planted in many gardens and parks
VINE *Vitis vinifera*
The occasional plant grows in parks and on waste ground. Probably from an office worker's lunch, as are many seedlings of fruit trees
LABURNUM *Laburnum anagyroides*
Widespread in parks and gardens, etc
BLACK MEDICK *Medicago lupulina*
Common in most parts of London. Lucerne (*M. sativa*) also occurs in many parts of London
CLOVERS *Trifolium* sp
The red clover *T. pratense* and white clover *T. repens* are very common in London. A few other species have been recorded, notably the alsike clover *T. hybridium*
BIRD'S-FOOT TREFOIL *Lotus corniculatus*
Found in several parks and open spaces in London
ACACIA *Robinia pseudoacacia*
Common in parks and gardens
VETCHES *Vicia* sp
Several species have been recorded from central London, the most frequently encountered being the hairy tare (*V. hirsuta*, the smooth tare (*V. tetrasperma*) and the tufted vetch (*V. cracca*)
CREEPING CINQUEFOIL *Potentilla reptans*
Common in most parts of London
CHERRY *Prunus avium*
Seedlings often spring up on waste ground, usually bird sown, but sometimes from human lunches
PLUM *P. domesticus*
Occasionally planted, seedlings often grow from stones discarded from office workers' lunches
ALMOND *P. amygdalus*
Frequently planted in parks, gardens and squares
HAWTHORN *Crataegus monogyna*
Abundant in parks, squares and gardens. Sometimes planted, other times occurring naturally
APPLE *Malus sylvestris*
A common 'lunch-escape' on waste ground
WILLOW HERBS *Epilobium* sp
The willow herbs can be described as being one of the characteristic groups of plants in London. Several species are common: the great hairy willow herb *E. hirsutum*, the broad-leaved willow herb *E. montanum* and the introduced *E. adenocaulon*. The small-flowered willow herb *E. parviflorum* is found in small numbers in Hyde Park and Kensington Gardens

ROSEBAY WILLOW HERB　*Chamaenerion angustifolium*
The most widespread and abundant of the willow herbs. The mauve of the rosebay willow herb together with the yellow of the ragwort are familiar on almost every area of waste ground in London
ENCHANTER'S NIGHTSHADE　*Circaea lutetiana*
Widespread; occurring as a weed in parks and gardens
SPIKED WATER-MILFOIL　*Myriophyllum spicatum*
Known from the Round Pond, Kensington Gardens
IVY　*Hedera helix*
In several parks, but not as widespread as might be expected
COW PARSLEY　*Anthriscus sylvestris*
Fairly widespread in the wilder areas of parks, along railway and canal embankments, etc
FOOL'S PARSLEY　*Aethusa cynapium*
Widespread. Occurs commonly as a weed in parks and gardens
HOGWEED　*Heracleum sphondylium*
Widespread. The giant hogweed (*H. mantegazzianum*), originally from the Caucasus, is also found in many parks and gardens
ANNUAL MERCURY　*Mercurialis annua*
Widespread. Found as a weed in parks and gardens, and also on waste ground
PETTY SPURGE　*Euphorbia peplus*
Widespread in parks and gardens as a weed
GRASSES　*Polygonum sp*
Several species are widespread: *P. aviculare*, *P. aequale*, *P. persicaria*, *P. convolvulus*, *P. baldschuanicum* and *P. cuspidatum*
SHEEP'S SORREL　*Rumex acetosella*
Occurs in several parks including Kensington Gardens
SORREL　*R. acetosa*
Widespread; occurs in most of the central parks
CURLED DOCK　*R. crispus*
Common
BROAD-LEAVED DOCK　*R. obtusifolius*
Common. Two other species of dock: the sharp dock *R. conglomeratus* and the red-veined dock *R. sanguineus* are also to be found in a few parks and open spaces
SMALL NETTLE　*Urtica urens*
Widespread; occurs as a weed in parks and gardens
STINGING NETTLE　*U. dioica*
Locally abundant; known from Regent's Park and Kensington Gardens
HEMP　*Cannabis sativa*
Occurs occasionally, growing from bird seed
ELM　*Ulmus procera*
Occurs in most of the parks

LONDON PLANE   *Platanus × hybrida*
Widespread in London. Planted in most parks and squares. Often in streets
SILVER BIRCH   *Betula pendula*
Planted in many of the parks and squares
ALDER   *Alnus glutinosa*
Occasionally planted in parks
HORNBEAM   *Carpinus betulus*
Occasionally planted in parks and squares
HAZEL   *Corylus avellana*
Occasionally planted and may spread naturally
OAK   *Quercus robur*
Planted in many parks. Other species of oak are also planted including the
Turkey oak *Q. cerris* and the sessile oak *Q. petraea*
SWEET CHESTNUT   *Castanea sativa*
Commonly planted in most parks and squares
BEECH   *Fagus sylvatica*
Most commonly found as hedges in central London
WILLOWS   *Salix* sp
Several species are planted in the parks, and the goat willow *S. caprea* is often
found in a wild state
WHITE POPLAR   *Populus alba*
An introduced species sometimes planted in parks and squares
ITALIAN BLACK POPLAR   *P. × canadensis*
A hybrid tree often planted in parks and squares
LOMBARDY POPLAR   *P. italica*
An introduced species occasionally planted
SCARLET PIMPERNEL   *Anagallis arvensis*
In most of the parks and also recorded from the Oval cricket ground
BUDDLIA   *Buddleia davidii*
An attractive garden plant of Chinese origin, which has colonised many
parts of London. It is particularly abundant in north London, St John's
Wood, Regent's Park, etc. Has also been recorded from Hyde Park and
Victoria
ASH   *Fraxinus excelsior*
Commonly planted in parks, squares and gardens
CORN BINDWEED   *Convolvulus arvensis*
Widespread
BINDWEEDS   *Calystegia* sp
The commonest species are *C. sepia* and *C. silvatica*. Although both occur well
into the centre of London, *C. silvatica* is rarer in the very central areas. The
results of a detailed survey of these species were published by E. B. Bangerter
in the *London Naturalist* (1967)

DUKE OF ARGYLL'S TEA-PLANT *Lycium halimifolium*
A garden plant which has been noted on waste ground; common on railway embankments near Paddington

DEADLY NIGHTSHADE *Atropa belladonna*
Rare. Has been recorded in central London, but not in the last two decades

TOMATO *Lycopersicon esculentum*
Fairly common on waste ground. Outside the central area, on the sewage farms, it is often extremely abundant

WOODY NIGHTSHADE *Solanum dulcamara*
Common; occurring as a weed in parks and gardens

BLACK NIGHTSHADE *S. nigrum*
Widespread and abundant in parks and gardens

POTATO *S. tuberosum*
Occasionally occurs, particularly along railway embankments

SPEEDWELLS *Veronica sp*
Several species have been recorded from central London, the most widespread being Buxbaum's speedwell (*V. persica*)

GIPSY-WORT *Lycopus europaeus*
Found on embankments close to water in several parts of central London, notably the Regent's Canal, River Thames and the Serpentine

HOREHOUND *Ballota nigra*
Common in many parts of London

HENBIT *Lamium amplexicaule*
Found in several central London parks and squares

RED DEAD-NETTLE *L. purpureum*
Widespread in central London, occurring as garden weed and on waste ground

WHITE DEAD-NETTLE *L. album*
Common and widespread

SKULL-CAP *Scutellaria galericulata*
Occurs only locally, on the Regent's Canal embankments

GREAT PLANTAIN *Plantago major*
Very common and widespread

RIBWORT *P. lanceolata*
Common in many parts of central London. Other species such as hoary plantain *P. media* and sea plantain *P. maritima* occasionally occur in imported turf in parks, golf courses, etc

GOOSEGRASS *Galium aparine*
Common and widespread

ELDER *Sambucus nigra*
Occurs on most waste ground. Seedlings often spring up in parks and gardens, usually introduced by birds

SUNFLOWER *Helianthus annuus*
Occasional, either as a garden escape or from bird seed
TRIPARTITE BUR-MARIGOLD *Bidens tripartita*
Occurs along Regent's Canal and the Thames embankments
GALLANT SOLDIER *Galinsoga parviflora*
A common alien, occurring as a weed in parks, gardens and squares. *G. ciliata*, a close relative, is particularly common around Mayfair, Chelsea, Kensington and along the Regent's Canal. Both these species are rare outside London
RAGWORTS *Senecio sp*
The ragwort *S. jacobaea* occurs in a few of the central parks occasionally, but it is the Oxford ragwort *S. squalidus*, originally found on volcanic hillsides in southern Europe, which has become one of the typical plants of London. The smaller species such as the groundsel *S. vulgaris* and the sticky groundsel *S. viscosus* are also well known as weeds of parks and gardens
COLTSFOOT *Tussilago farfara*
Common and widespread
MARIGOLD *Calendula officinalis*
Originally from southern Europe, this popular garden species is often well established on waste ground, railway embankments, etc
GOLDEN ROD *Solidago sp*
A garden escape which is often abundant on waste ground
MICHAELMAS DAISY *Aster sp*
Several species of Michaelmas daisy, all of which are garden escapes, are often found on waste ground. The most common is *A. novi-belgii*, but *A. novae-angliae* and *A. lanceolatus* are also quite common
CANADIAN FLEABANE *Conyza canadensis*
Common and widespread
DAISY *Bellis perennis*
Common and widespread, occurring in lawns in parks and gardens
YARROW *Achillea millefolium*
Common in many parts of central London
SCENTLESS MAYWEED *Tripleurospermum maritimum*
Common and widespread
WILD CHAMOMILE *Matricaria recutita*
Common in parks and gardens
RAYLESS MAYWEED *M. matricaroides*
Common on open waste ground and alongside paths
FEVERFEW *Chrysanthemum parthenium*
Originally from the Balkans, occurs as a garden escape in Hyde Park, Green Park and a few other places
MUGWORT *Artemisia vulgaris*
Common on waste ground. Another interesting species, *A. verlotorum*, originally

Page 143 (*above*) Lichens can be very useful indicators of pollution levels (see p 66). In this picture a growth of *Caloplaca heppiana* is growing on an eighteenth-century headstone in St Lawrence's churchyard, Morden; (*below*) spotted orchid growing on open grassland at Boxhill, Surrey

Page 144 (*above*) Muntjac deer are an introduction which have successfully colonised several parts of Britain; there are thriving colonies in Hertfordshire, and it is quite possible that they will spread into the suburbs of London; (*below*) sika deer exist in the wild state in several parts of Britain; around London they are normally confined to parks, such as this herd in Knowle Park, Sevenoaks, but occasionally escapes occur and the animals may breed in the wild

from China, is common in several parts of central London, particularly south of the Thames

LESSER BURDOCK *Arctium minus*
Common on most waste ground

SPEAR THISTLE *Cirsium vulgare*
Widespread on the larger areas of waste ground and in large gardens

CREEPING THISTLE *C. arvense*
Very common

CORNFLOWER *Centaurea cyanus*
Occasionally occurs, but usually in the cultivated form

KNAPWEED *C. nigra*
Found in damp places in some of the squares and parks

NIPPLEWORT *Lapsana communis*
Common and widespread

COMMON CAT'S EAR *Hypochoeris radicata*
Common. Often occurring as a weed in parks and gardens

SMOOTH HAWKBIT *Leontodon autumnalis*
Common in many parts of central London, elsewhere in Britain is often found on mountains

CORN SOWTHISTLE *Sonchus arvensis*
Fairly common, occurring as a weed in parks and gardens

COMMON SOWTHISTLE *S. oleraceus*
An abundant and widespread weed in parks and gardens. The prickly sow-thistle *S. Asper* also occurs in Hyde Park, Kensington Gardens and a few other localities

HAWK'S BEARD *Crepis sp*
Both the beaked hawk's beard *C. vesicaria* and the smooth hawk's beard *C. capillaris* are found in a few localities in central London

DANDELION *Taraxacum officinale*
Very common

POND WEEDS *Potamogeton sp*
The Round Pond in Kensington Gardens is one of the best localities for this genus, the small pondweed *P. pusillus*, the curled pondweed *P. crispus* and the fennel-like pondweed *P. pectinatus* all having been recorded. The latter two species are also known from the Regent's Canal

HORNED PONDWEED *Zannichellia palustris*
Known from the Round Pond, Kensington Gardens

RUSHES *Juncus sp*
Kensington Gardens is one of the best localities in central London, the slender rush *J. tenuis*, the toad rush *J. bufonius* and the soft rush *J. effusus* all having been recorded

SEDGES *Carex sp*
Several species have been recorded from central London though none are

I

abundant. The hairy sedge *C. hirta* is probably the most widespread and has been recorded from Hyde Park, Kensington Gardens and St James's Park

FESCUES *Festuca* sp

Many species have been recorded but none can be considered widespread or common

RYE GRASS *Lolium perenne*

Common and widespread

ITALIAN RYE GRASS *L. multiflorum*

Common and widespread

ANNUAL MEADOWGRASS *Poa annua*

One of the most abundant grasses everywhere

MEADOW GRASS *P. pratensis*

Common and widespread. Several other species are also found in central London, including the narrow-leaved meadow grass *P. angustifolia*, the rough meadow grass *P. trivialis* and the marsh meadow grass *P. palustris*

COCK'S FOOT *Dactylis glomerata*

Common and widespread mainly in the parks

COUCH GRASS *Agropyron repens*

Common and widespread, often occurring as a garden weed

WILD BARLEY *Hordeum murinum*

Very common on waste ground

YORKSHIRE FOG *Holcus lanatus*

Fairly widespread in the central parks

COMMON BENT *Agrostis tenuis*

Common and widespread

CREEPING BENT *A. stolonifera*

Common and widespread. Hybrids between this species and *A. tenuis* are common

TIMOTHY *Phleum pratense*

Fairly widespread, occurring in most of the central parks

MEADOW FOXTAIL *Alopecurus pratensis*

Common in lawns, parks and squares

CANARY GRASS *Phalaris canariensis*

Occasionally occurs, introduced with bird seed. Has been found in Piccadilly and near the Festival Hall

MILLET *Panicum miliaceum*

Occasionally grows in gardens, parks, squares and even window boxes from bird seed

Mammals

Since most mammals are only rarely seen, all those recorded in the last five years are included in this list, excluding marine mammals. The list follows that in *The Identification of British Mammals* (1964) by G. B. Corbet, published by the British Museum (Natural History). As with the birds, the term 'throughout London' should always be qualified by 'where suitable habitat is available'.

HEDGEHOG *Erinaceus europaeus*
Widespread throughout most of London except the centre. Very abundant in the outer suburbs

MOLE *Talpa europaea*
Rarely seen, but its presence is easily detected by the conspicuous mole hills. Rare in the suburbs. Confined to large parks in the outer suburbs and to rural areas

COMMON SHREW *Sorex araneus*
Confined to the outer suburbs and beyond, where it is abundant

PYGMY SHREW *S. minutus*
Known only from the outer suburban and rural areas. Much less abundant than the common shrew, though fairly widely distributed

WATER SHREW *Neomys fodiens*
Occurs mainly in rural areas in unpolluted rivers and streams, though is often found a considerable distance from water. Watercress beds are a favourite haunt of this species

BATS
The whiskered bat *Myotis mystacinus*, Natterer's bat *M. nattereri*, Brandt's bat *M. brandti* and Daubenton's bat *M. daubentoni* are known to occur in the rural areas on the outskirts of south London. Most of the observations on them have been made in derelict mines in the Godstone and Westerham areas

SEROTINE BAT *Eptesicus serotinus*
A fairly widespread species occurring in many of the outer suburbs. Is more frequently recorded than the similar noctule bat, because it more frequently roosts in houses—the noctule prefers trees. Can be seen at Rye Meads sewage farm and Godstone Ponds among other places

LEISLER'S BAT   *Nyctalus leisleri*
Generally considered rare, but has been recorded from Kew and Walton-on-Thames among other places

NOCTULE BAT   *N. noctula*
Widespread in the outer suburbs, often feeding over rubbish tips. Easily confused with the two previous species. Can be seen, with several other species, feeding over Godstone Ponds

PIPISTRELLE   *Pipistrellus pipistrellus*
Regarded as commonest bat but the few accurate identifications make it impossible to assess its distribution. Probably occurs well into suburban and even urban areas

LONG-EARED BAT   *Plecotus auritus*
Fairly widespread but nowhere common. Only recorded in fairly rural areas

FOX   *Vulpes vulpes*
Widespread and abundant in the outer suburbs. A few occur in the inner suburbs, particularly near areas of waste ground, parks, etc

STOAT   *Mustela erminea*
Widespread in larger parks and commons in the outer suburbs but rare in Middlesex

WEASEL   *M. nivalis*
Shows a similar distribution to the previous species, but is found further in towards the centre of London, is always more abundant, and is found in a few localities in Middlesex

BADGER   *Meles meles*
Abundant in the rural areas surrounding London, particularly in Kent. Also found in many of the outer suburbs where it will visit gardens to feed regularly. The setts at Richmond Park and Putney are probably the nearest to central London

ROE DEER   *Capreolus capreolus*
Occurs in Surrey and has been spreading in towards London over the previous decade. Has been seen in suburban gardens. Known to occur on Bookham Common, Fetcham Down and in the Stoke D'Abernon area

FALLOW DEER   *Dama dama*
Epping Forest has a well-established herd of fallow deer. Park herds can be seen in many London parks, such as Richmond (with red deer), Greenwich and Battersea. A small herd exists in a wild state in Lullingstone Park

MUNTJAC DEER   *Muntiacus* sp
This introduced species is particularly abundant in woods around Potters Bar, Herts, and may well spread and establish itself in the London suburbs. Other species of deer, such as the sika, can be seen in parks and occasionally escape. Although there are no positive records, Chinese water deer could well be seen too.

RED DEER *Cervus elaphus*
A park deer, notably in Richmond, but for some years escapes have been seen in the Chessington area

HARE *Lepus capensis*
Widespread in the countryside around London. Occurs in Richmond Park but in few other areas within the suburbs

RABBIT *Oryctolagus cuniculus*
Widespread in the outer suburbs and in larger parks, commons, etc

GREY SQUIRREL *Sciurus carolinensis*
Introduced around the turn of the century, this species is well established in almost every open space in the London suburbs and absent only from the very heart of the built-up area

RED SQUIRREL *S. vulgaris*
Formerly widespread in London, last recorded from Epping Forest in 1957 and 1959. It is generally a popular animal and very likely that someone will try to re-establish it one day

DORMOUSE *Muscardinus avellanarius*
Overlooked for many years, this species has recently been recorded in rural areas bordering the outer suburbs in Kent and Surrey

HARVEST MOUSE *Micromys minutus*
Found in many rural areas around London including Bookham Common and Rye Meads sewage farm

WOOD MOUSE *Apodemus sylvaticus*
Abundant and widespread in the outer suburban areas, where it often comes into houses in the winter

YELLOW-NECKED MOUSE *A. flavicollis*
Known only from Kent and Surrey, bordering the London suburbs. Fairly common around Esher/Oxshott/Hersham/Weybridge area

HOUSE MOUSE *Mus musculus*
An urban animal, abundant in the centre of London but often rare in the outer suburbs

BLACK RAT *Rattus rattus*
Once an abundant pest throughout England is now quite a rare animal. Occurs in the West End (Oxford Street), the Port of London and a few other areas. Is possibly one of Britain's rarest animals—but no one is likely to bring in protection

BROWN RAT *R. norvegicus*
Abundant and widespread throughout the urban, suburban and rural areas

BANK VOLE *Clethrionomys glareolus*
Widespread in hedgerows and woods in the outer suburbs

WATER VOLE *Arvicola terrestris*
Fairly widespread on suitable rivers. Most abundant in Middlesex on River Colne and tributaries

FIELD VOLE *Microtus agrestis*

Found on unmown commons and parks throughout the suburbs. Occasionally populations build up and attract large numbers of predators. This is most obvious at Beddington sewage farm, Surrey

Reptiles and amphibians

SMOOTH NEWT *Triturus vulgaris*
The commonest species of newt in London. Occurs in ponds, lakes and ditches throughout the outer suburbs of London, often in ornamental and garden ponds
PALMATE NEWT *T. helveticus*
The species has a fairly restricted distribution around London. Common in Epping Forest, Essex; Farningham Wood, Kent and Bookham Common, Surrey
CRESTED NEWT *T. cristatus*
Rarer than the two previous species but found in odd places throughout the outer suburbs. Rare in Epping Forest, Essex; fairly abundant Bookham Common, Surrey
COMMON FROG *Rana temporaria*
This species is apparently declining in the London area, due no doubt to the filling in of ponds and ditches as suburbia spreads. The collection and transportation of spawn may drastically alter distribution
EDIBLE FROG *R. esculenta*
This species is not a native of Britain but has been introduced on several occasions. No thriving colonies are known now. Formerly occurred in Epping Forest, Hampstead Heath and Esher and Ham Commons
COMMON TOAD *Bufo bufo*
This species has a similar distribution to that of the common frog, but is generally more widespread. Toads tend to return to ancestral ponds and are often killed on roads
COMMON LIZARD *Lacerta vivipara*
Common in the countryside around London and survives in small numbers in pockets throughout the suburbs. Has been found on Wimbledon Common, Beddington sewage farm and Bookham Common, Surrey; Epping Forest, Essex; around Brent reservoir, Middlesex and many other localities
SLOW WORM *Anguis fragilis*
Widely distributed, found in many suburban parks and often common in outer suburbia. Areas it has been recorded from include Epping Forest, Essex; Plumstead, Sydenham and Shoreham, Kent; Bookham Common and Esher area, Surrey

GRASS SNAKE   *Natrix natrix*
Although fairly widespread in rural areas around London, very rare in the suburbs

ADDER   *Vipera berus*
Fairly common in the rural areas around London such as Epping Forest or Esher Common. Usually rather localised, no doubt due to persecution by the inhabitants of the adjacent suburbia

Other reptiles and amphibians are occasionally found and large numbers are imported into Britain as pets. Some of these escape or are released. Records of such animals in London include the tree frog *Hyla arborea*, the terrapin *Emys obicularis*, the green lizard *Lacerta viridis* sp and wall lizard *L. muralis* sp

Natural history societies

THERE ARE MANY such natural history societies centred on London; below is a list of some of the more important:

Botanical Society of the British Isles,
c/o British Museum (Natural History),
Cromwell Road,
London, SW7

Institute of Biology,
41 Queen's Gate,
London, SW7

Linnean Society,
Burlington House,
Piccadilly,
London, W1

Royal Entomological Society,
41 Queen's Gate,
London, SW7

Society for the Promotion of Nature Reserves,
c/o British Museum (Natural History),
Cromwell Road,
London, SW7

Zoological Society of London,
Regent's Park,
London, NW1

This is a selection of local natural history societies. The addresses can be obtained from the Council for Nature, Zoological Gardens, Regent's Park, London, NW1.

British Entomological & Natural History Society
Croydon Natural History Society
Epping Forest Field Centre
Essex Birdwatching & Preservation Society
Essex Field Club
Hampstead Scientific Society
Juniper Hall Field Centre (Box Hill)
Kent Ornithological Society
London Natural History Society
Ruislip & District Natural History Society
South London Botanical Institute
South Essex Natural History Society

Places to visit

A SHORT LIST of places mentioned in the text, together with a few others. A very approximate national grid reference (four figure) is given, indicating the smallest squares on the one-inch Ordnance Survey maps.

ABBEY WOOD (TQ 4878)
This wood and the adjacent Bortall Wood and Lesnes Abbey Wood have a fine spring flora. Geologists must obtain prior permission in order to dig (see Appendix Four)

AVERY HILL (TQ 4474)
A small park in the outer suburbs sometimes described as a mini-Kew

BANSTEAD WOODS (TQ 2657)
Typical North Downs woodland. Brambling often abundant in winter

BARN ELMS RESERVOIRS (TQ 2277)
Situated just south of the Thames, a few minutes' walk from Hammersmith station, these reservoirs are certainly worth a visit by ornithologists. Permit from Metropolitan Water Board

BATTERSEA PARK (TQ 2877)
Between Albert Bridge and Chelsea Bridge, has a small zoo, herd of fallow deer, dolphinarium, and collection of ornamental waterfowl

BECKENHAM PLACE PARK (TQ 3870)
A typical large suburban park

BEDDINGTON SEWAGE FARM (TQ 2866)
One of the better-known haunts of London's birdwatchers. Also interesting lichens—adjacent to the sewage farm is St Mary's church, Beddington, the wall of which has a good collection. Mitcham Common and Beddington Park border the farm. Permit needed from the Manager, Beddington Lane, Mitcham, Surrey

BELAIR—see DULWICH WOODS

BIGGIN WOODS—see DULWICH WOODS

BLACKHEATH (TQ 2866)
Once one of the finest examples of heath around London, but sadly, now largely football pitches. A few stunted gorse bushes serve to remind the visitor of its former glory. The gravels of the Thames terraces can be seen. In spring and autumn, passage migrants occur in some numbers

BLOOMSBURY SQUARE (TQ 3081)
One of many squares to be found in central London, characterised by exotic trees, but often with a remarkable amount of indigenous wildlife

BOOKHAM COMMON (TQ 1256)
The London Natural History Society maintains a research centre for studying the ecology of the commons and woods. One of the best documented areas around London (and the rest of Britain)

BOX HILL (TQ 1751)
One of the classic chalk downland habitats, with a splendid flora and interesting fauna. Well worth a visit, particularly in mid-summer. Juniper Hall Field Centre, close by, runs many courses on local natural history

BRENT (WELSH HARP) RESERVOIR (TQ 2187)
Lies next to the A5 (Watling Street) in the suburbs. Attracts a wide variety of birds, and is particularly good in autumn

BUSHY PARK (TQ 1569)
A large park into which cars may be taken. Has herd of red deer

CHALDON (TQ 3155)
Good chalk downland, outstanding for molluscs. The local church is worth a visit to see a little-known medieval wall painting of hell

CHARLTON PIT (TQ 4178)
Of interest to geologists, this pit shows one of the finest exposures of the Lower Eocene/Lower Tertiary beds in the London area

CHELSEA PHYSIC GARDEN (TQ 2777)
Just along from Cheyne Walk, the physic garden is an early botanical collection dealing with plants of medicinal value. Not normally open to the public, but can be viewed by appointment

CRYSTAL PALACE PARK (TQ 3470)
The site of the 'Crystal Palace' buildings of the great exhibition of 1851, which were later re-erected here, but were burnt down in 1936. The high ground gives a good view over London. Around the boating lake there is a collection of reconstructions of fossil dinosaurs, etc, which were made under the supervision of Richard Owen, the first director of the Natural History Museum

CUMMING MUSEUM (TQ 3278)
A small local museum in the Walworth Road with some interesting specimens

DEVILSDEN WOODS (TQ 3057)
Another good example of chalk downland and woodland

DULWICH WOODS AND PARK (TQ 3472)
The woods form an unspoilt oasis in the suburbs. A permit is needed to visit (from The Estates Governors of Dulwich College) but much of the area can be seen from Cox's Walk and other public paths. Biggin Woods (TQ 3170) and Grange Wood (TQ 3268) are public parks, and are relics of the Great North Wood at one time connected to Dulwich Wood. Woodland birds and spring

flowers are the main attractions. Dulwich Park and Belair House are also worth a visit

EPPING FOREST (TQ 4298)
A popular recreation spot for Londoners, it is still one of the wildest places around London. The many ponds are of particular interest, also the flora, the fungi and the herd of wild fallow deer

ESHER COMMON (TQ 1262)
A typical Surrey common

GEOLOGICAL SURVEY MUSEUM (TQ 2679)
One of the South Kensington museums, dealing mainly with the geology of the British Isles

GODSTONE PONDS (TQ 3552)
Visit on a summer evening, when four or more species of bat can always be seen

GREEN PARK (TQ 2879)
One of the least interesting of the central London parks

GREENWICH PARK (TQ 3877)
Ajoins Blackheath, and is close to some of London's finest buildings. Has herd of fallow deer

HAMPSTEAD HEATH (TQ 2686)
A popular spot which somehow manages to retain most of its natural beauty and a fair amount of its wildlife

HAMPTON COURT PARK (TQ 1668)
Situated around Hampton Court Palace, it contains a variety of habitats ranging from formal gardens and ponds to rough meadows

HAREFIELD GREAT PIT (TQ 0408)
Situated on the outskirts of London this is one of the classic sites for geologists. Permit needed from W. W. Drinkwater (Willesden) Ltd, Dudden Hill Lane, London, NW10

HEATHROW AIRPORT (TQ 0775)
The point of entry and exit for many of London's visitors. In winter golden plover can be seen and also hares

HERSHAM SEWAGE FARM (TQ 1265)
A small sewage farm regularly watched and studied by an active ringing group

HIGHGATE WOODS (TQ 2888)
Situated close to Hampstead Heath, Highgate and Queen's Wood are one of the few relatively unspoilt areas of woodland in the north London suburbs

HOLLAND PARK (TQ 2479)
Situated a couple of minutes' walk from High Street, Kensington, parts of Holland Park are remarkably wild and support a wide variety of woodland birds. In the more formal gardens of Holland House peacocks and jungle fowl give an exotic atmosphere

HORNIMAN MUSEUM (TQ 3473)
A remarkable museum at Forest Hill, SE23. The building itself is a fine example

of art nouveau architecture and the collections include a vivarium and aquarium. Known for well-illustrated lectures on Saturday afternoons and some evenings

HOSEY COMMON (TQ 4552)

A good heathland flora. Woodcock, nightjar, tree pipit and wood warbler breed

HYDE PARK (TQ 2780)

One of the largest of the central London parks. Ajoins Kensington Gardens, and the Serpentine attracts a variety of waterfowl including a flock of Canada geese which flight between the central London parks

KENWOOD (TQ 2787)

Approached over Hampstead Heath. Kenwood has many attractions, not least are the open-air concerts held in the quiet woodland setting during the summer months

KESTON COMMON (TQ 4165)

An interesting common with a particularly interesting pond flora

KING GEORGE V RESERVOIR (TQ 3695)

One of the largest of the Lea Valley reservoirs; visit for wintering waterfowl. Permit needed from Metropolitan Water Board

KING GEORGE VI RESERVOIR (TQ 0473)

Permit needed from the Metropolitan Water Board. One of the most important localities for waterfowl in the London area

LIMPSFIELD COMMON (TQ 4052)

A typical Surrey common, good for summer migrant birds

LONDON MUSEUM (TQ 2580)

In Kensington Palace, this museum has exhibits on many of the historical and archaeological aspects of London

LONSDALE ROAD RESERVOIRS (TQ 2277)

Close to Barn Elms reservoirs, these are largely overgrown and drained, but still worth a visit

LULLINGSTONE PARK (TQ 5164)

A fine area of parkland, surrounded by agricultural land. Holds a wide variety of birds. Badgers are common, also harvest mice. The nearby River Darenth and its tributaries contain crayfish. The famous Roman villa is certainly worth a visit

MITCHAM COMMON (TQ 2868)

A large common in the suburbs which joins on to Beddington Sewage Farm

NATURAL HISTORY MUSEUM—BRITISH MUSEUM (NATURAL HISTORY) (TQ 2679)

One of the world's most important collections. The public galleries are being modernised and contain some interesting specimens

NORTHAW GREAT WOOD (TL 2802)

Situated well outside London near Cuffley, Northaw is a wild area of woodland and is the best locality around London for seeing muntjac deer

OTFORD (TQ 5259)
A relatively unspoilt stretch of the River Darenth in which a variety of fish as well as crayfish can be found. Snipe, water voles, and other interesting wildlife are to be found in the adjacent water meadows

PRIMROSE HILL (TQ 2783)
One of the highest spots in north London. A good place for watching migrant birds in autumn

PUTNEY HEATH (TQ 2373)
Together with Wimbledon Common it forms a large area of fairly unspoilt heathland close to the centre of London

QUEEN ELIZABETH II RESERVOIR (TQ 1167)
The largest of the Molesey group of reservoirs. Permit needed from Metropolitan Water Board

QUEEN MARY RESERVOIR (TQ 0769)
The largest of London's reservoirs. Attracts vast numbers of gulls as well as other water birds

RAINHAM MARSH (TQ 5280)
The main attraction is the concentration of waders and duck, particularly in autumn and winter

REGENT'S PARK (TQ 2782)
A large park surrounded by the famous Nash Terraces. London Zoo, on the north side of the park, has one of the largest collections of animals in the world

RICHMOND PARK (TQ 1972)
The largest of the Royal Parks, has herds of both red and fallow deer. Tree pipits and a variety of other birds breed. Visit the Isabella Plantation (in spring for the azaleas) and the Pen Ponds

RUISLIP (TQ 0889)
Around Ruislip there are several areas of interest to naturalists including a nature reserve

RUXLEY GRAVEL PIT (TQ 4970)
An overgrown gravel pit visited mainly by birdwatchers

RYE MEADS (TL 3910)
Well out of London, an important bird ringing and observation station operates on the sewage farm

ST JAMES'S PARK (TQ 2979)
The most central of London's parks. Has a good collection of waterfowl, which often attract wild duck

STAINES RESERVOIR (TQ 0472)
Next to King George VI reservoir. No permit needed as there is a public footpath along the causeway running across the reservoir. One of the most important sites in Britain for water birds, including the rarer gulls, terns, grebes and duck. Staines Moor is also worth a visit

STOKE NEWINGTON RESERVOIRS (TQ 3288)
The reservoirs can be observed from the aqueduct bridge and between railings
on the north side. During hard weather vast concentrations of duck and other
waterfowl occur. Notable for smew

SURREY DOCKS AND THAMES (TQ 3680)
Recent studies have shown that large numbers of duck are wintering on the
Thames here. Best viewed from a boat

TOOTING BEC AND GRAVENEY COMMONS (TQ 2871)
Typical suburban commons. Ponds well-stocked with fish

WALTHAMSTOW RESERVOIRS (TQ 3588)
Part of the Lea Valley complex of reservoirs. Famous for the heronry

WALTON HEATH (TQ 2253)
Near many other Surrey heaths and commons, this is probably the best one
for birds

WILLIAM GIRLING RESERVOIR (TQ 3694)
Close to, but less interesting than, King George V reservoir

WIMBLEDON COMMON (TQ 2271)
Close to central London and well worth a visit for most aspects of natural
history

How to find mammals

THROUGHOUT THE BOOK I have made little attempt to explain any of the methods used in finding, observing and identifying London's wildlife. Of all living nature—mammals, birds, flowers, insects, reptiles—the study of mammals presents the most difficulty. They are shy, often nocturnal, sometimes living almost entirely underground, so that discovering them involves a fascinating element of detective work. This appendix is intended as a rough guide to such investigations.

Mammals can be studied in several different ways in and around London:

Field observations

Badgers can be watched at the sett, and there is always a chance of seeing foxes and rabbits at the same time. Bats can often be seen hawking for insects at twilight but they are almost impossible to identify accurately in the field. Weasels and stoats are often seen by ornithologists as readily as by mammalogists, probably because the latter tend to do their field work with their eyes to the ground whereas birdwatchers are looking in the middle distance and consequently see the stoats and weasels!

Trapping

Since small mammals are, on the whole, difficult to observe, methods of study other than direct observation are usually employed. The most obvious method is trapping, but break-back mousetraps are unnecessarily destructive and live traps such as the Longworth Trap are not only expensive but require a considerable amount of time and effort to produce results. For detailed studies and surveys live traps are almost essential and apart from Longworth's there are several other traps which can either be purchased or improvised with a little ingenuity; but for most naturalists a more efficient method of recording the mammal's presence in an area is needed if only one or two visits are possible. Trapping needs to be carried out over several weeks, ideally.

Examination of bird pellets

One of the most interesting methods is to examine the food remains of birds of prey. Most species of predatory birds including owls, falcons, gulls and herons regurgitate pellets of the undigested matter in their prey. Since owls, kestrels and other species often adopt a particular perch as a roost these pellets accumulate and can be collected and examined. From them an accurate idea of not only the predator's diet, but also of the prey animals present in the neighbourhood can be gained. The pellets vary in size and shape depending on the species and consist of fur, feathers, bones, teeth, wing cases of insects, etc, and can be dissected with a needle and a pair of forceps. Sometimes the remains are difficult to identify but mammalian skulls are remarkably durable, often emerging almost complete, and are easily identifiable with the aid of a key. Good keys are to be found in *The Identification of British Mammals* by G. B. Corbet and *Mammals of Britain, Their Tracks, Trails and Signs* by M. J. Lawrence and R. W. Brown.

Examination of discarded bottles

Another method of recording mammals is of relatively recent discovery; it involves searching for discarded bottles. This amazingly unlikely method was first used scientifically by the mammalogists Pat Morris and John Harper. It depends on the fact that mammals enter bottles, presumably in the course of exploring their territory, and exit is prevented for a number of reasons—shape, neck, size and the position of the bottle being the most important. A small mammal, such as a shrew or mouse, can squeeze into the bottle by pushing with its feet on the ground outside; once in, however, particularly if the bottle is pointing slightly upwards, the mammal has nothing but the sloping smooth sides of the bottle to anchor against. The inside of the bottle is often wet and this tends to stick the mammal's fur to the glass and very soon the animal, unable to escape, dies. The corpse attracts beetles, flies and other insects which may in turn provide a further attraction for other small mammals, and not infrequently the remains of several individuals of several species may be found in varying states of putrefaction. Even when completely decomposed so that only a skeleton survives, the remains can be readily identified with the aid of the same keys used for identifying remains from bird pellets. It should be pointed out that this method is not to be recommended to the squeamish or to anyone with a sensitive sense of smell.

The best places to find bottles are around the areas visited by picnickers and resting motorists. Roadside laybys and railway embankments are two of the finest hunting grounds. Very often large numbers of discarded milk, beer, wine and other types of bottle are to be found in the bushes and vegetation surrounding a layby. But remember, searching for discarded bottles not only sometimes looks suspicious but, as the author has found out, can even require a practical demonstration to a police patrol!

Tracks and other signs

Tracks and other signs can often be very helpful in indicating the whereabouts of mammals, particularly the larger species. Footprints and spraints are usually characteristic and other features such as fraying stocks (deer), nuts which have been split or gnawed (squirrels and mice), hair caught on barbed wire (badgers and foxes), are all equally helpful. When surveying badgers in the London area most of the information was collected without a badger actually being seen. The large mounds outside the sett indicated its presence and then its occupation was established by footprints, fresh dung, new footpaths, etc. Foxes could often be detected in badger setts, and elsewhere, by their distinctive odour. Moles are another species hardly ever actually seen, but the 'tumps' or molehills are very obvious.

Corpses

Finding dead mammals can provide useful information but, in general, animals soon disappear once they are dead, although very occasionally a dead weasel or shrew may be found on a path. During a myxomatosis epidemic dead and dying rabbits will be strewn across the countryside, but normally the road-sides produce the greatest number of corpses. The peak mortality is usually late summer, when the young are dispersing. In the suburbs, squirrels and hedge-hogs are the usual victims with the occasional rat, further out almost any animal from deer to weasel and hare to badger is likely to be killed on the roads. Roads are also a hazard to many other forms of wildlife—in spring, in particular, when birds are feeding young many birds are killed there.

APPENDIX FOUR

Collecting fossils

MANY OF THE localities mentioned are classified as Sites of Special Scientific Interest (SSSI) and a permit is necessary to visit them. Application should be made to the Chief Parks Officer, GLC Parks Dept, Cavell House, 2A Charing Cross Road, London WC2. Casual visitors to most sites are allowed to sift the spoil heaps, the main exposures in some cases being reserved for scientific research work.

Although many of the exposures around London have been visited many times by geologists new data is constantly being produced by improved research methods. For this reason it is vital that pits and other sites should be kept in good condition. This can be done by regular visiting, careful collecting, making detailed notes, keeping the exposures clear of screes and talus slopes for other geologists and immediately reporting any damage such as dumping.

Further reading

INCLUDED THROUGHOUT THIS list are a number of books which, although of more than local interest, provide useful background material for anyone who wishes to study wildlife in the London area. There are hundreds of books on Britain's natural history; this selection even with regard to London, must therefore be considered a personal choice. In the case of papers published in periodicals, it is even more difficult to make a selection. By and large, the choice here is restricted to those papers constantly referred to while researching this book; there are many others of importance.

GENERAL

Bevan, G. 'Twenty Five years of the Bookham Common Survey and Bibliography of the Natural History of Bookham Common, Surrey', *London Naturalist*, 43 (1964), 95–102

Butler, R. E. 'The Buried Rivers of London', *London Naturalist*, 41 (1962), 31–41

Chandler, T. J. *The Climate of London* (1965)

Fitter, R. S. R. *London's Natural History* (New Naturalist Series, 1945)

Fleure, H. J. and Davies, M. *A Natural History of Man in Britain* (New Naturalist Series, 1951, revised 1971). A good general account of man's impact in Britain as a whole—particularly relevant in these over populated days

Lousley, J. E. 'Dulwich Woods: Relics of the Great North Woods', *London Naturalist*, 39 (1959), 77–90

Stamp, L. Dudley. *Britain's Structure and Scenery* (New Naturalist Series, 1947)

Woodley, G. M. 'The London Thames and the Changing Levels of the Land and Sea', *London Naturalist*, 40 (1961), 115–20

The publications of the British Entomological & Natural History Society (formerly the South London Entomological & Natural History Society) contain a wealth of information, particularly concerning insects and invertebrates of the London area.

BIRDS

Brown, E. P. 'The Bird Life of Holland Park, 1962–3', *London Bird Report*, 28 (1964), 69–78

Cramp, S. 'The Census of Swifts, Swallows and House Martins, 1949', *London Bird Report*, 14 (1950), 49–57

Fitter, R. S. R. *London's Birds* (1949). A useful book for anyone interested in the history of birds in London

Gibbs, A. 'The Bird Population of Rubbish Dumps', *London Bird Report*, 26 (1963), 104–10

Gladwin, T. W. 'A Short Account of Rye Meads, Herts, and its Ornithology', *London Bird Report*, 26 (1963), 88–99

Gooders, J. *Where to Watch Birds* (1967). Gives good coverage to places within easy reach of London

Harting, J. E. *The Birds of Middlesex* (1866). Long out of print and difficult to find, but well worth reading

Heinzel, H., Fitter, R. S. R. and Parslow, J. L. F. *Birds of Britain and Europe* (1972). The most recent field guide, in full colour and with first-class maps

Hudson, W. H. *Birds in London* (1898, reprinted Newton Abbot 1969). A classic of ornithological writing

Hutson, A., Burton, J. A. and Stephens, S. D. G. 'Some preliminary Results of Swift Ringing at Beddington Sewage Farm, Surrey', *London Bird Report*, 35 (1970), 81–7

London Natural History Society (members of). *Birds of the London Area* (originally New Naturalist Series, 1957; reprinted and revised Rupert Hart-Davis 1964)

Montier, D. 'A Survey of the Breeding Distribution of the Kestrel, Barn Owl and Tawny Owl in the London Area in 1967', *London Bird Report*, 32 (1968), 81–92

Murton, R. K. *Man and Birds* (New Naturalist Series, 1972)

Nau, B. S. 'Sand Martin Colonies in the London Area', *London Bird Report*, 25 (1961), 69–81

Pentelow, F. T. K. 'The Lake in St James's Park', *London Naturalist*, 44 (1965), 128–37

Sage, Bryan L. 'The Breeding Distribution of the Tree Sparrow', *London Bird Report*, 27 (1963), 56–65

Sage, Bryan L. 'The Gull Roosts of the London Area', *London Bird Report*, 28 (1964), 63–8

Scott, Peter. *A Coloured Key to the Wildfowl of the World* (Wildfowl Trust, 1950; many reprints). A useful little book which should enable the observer to identify the many exotic ducks and geese to be seen in London's parks

Simms, Eric. *Woodland Birds* (New Naturalist Series, 1972)

Swann, H. K. *The Birds of London* (1893). A little known work which contains considerably more information than Hudson's book

FISH, REPTILES AND AMPHIBIANS

Burrett, John. *Freshwater Fishing the Lower Thames* (1960). As its title suggests, this is an anglers' guide

Meadows, B. S. 'Observations on the Return of Fishes to a Polluted Tributary of the River Thames, 1964–69', *London Naturalist*, 49 (1970), 76–81

Muus, Bent J. and Dahlstrøm, Preben. *Freshwater Fish of Britain and Europe* (1972). An identification guide, well illustrated

Smith, Malcolm. *British Reptiles and Amphibians* (New Naturalist Series, 1951; revised 1954). A very comprehensive work

Wheeler, A. C. 'Fishes of the London Area', *London Naturalist*, 37 (1957), 80–101

Yalden, D. W. 'Distribution of Reptiles and Amphibians in the London Area', *London Naturalist*, 44 (1965), 57–69

FLORA

Bangerter, E. B. 'A Survey of Calystegia in the London Area, Fifth and Final Report', *London Naturalist*, 46 (1967), 15–23

Clapham, A. R. et al. *Flora of the British Isles* (Cambridge University Press, many editions). A standard handbook, but difficult for the beginner to use

Jones, A. W. 'The Flora of the City of London Bombed Sites', *London Naturalist*, 37 (1957), 189–211

Lange, M. and Hora, F. B. *Collin's Guide to Mushrooms and Toadstools* (1963). A useful identification guide

Laundon, J. R. 'London's Lichens', *London Naturalist*, 49 (1970), 20–68

Lousley, J. E. *Wild Flowers of Chalk and Limestone* (New Naturalist Series, 1950). Discusses the flora of the North Downs in detail

Keble-Martin, W. *A Concise British Flora* (1965). A triumph of botanical illustration, also one of the best books for identifying flowering plants

Payne, R. M. 'The Ferns of Epping Forest', *London Naturalist*, 39 (1960), 25–30

Step, E. *Wayside and Woodland Trees* (1904). Still probably the best pocket book, though out of print

Whitton, B. A. 'Algae in St James's Park Lake', *London Naturalist*, 45 (1966), 26–8

INSECTS, OTHER INVERTEBRATES, FOSSILS

Groves, E. W. 'Some Entomological Records from the Cripplegate Bombed Sites, City of London', *London Naturalist*, 38 (1959), 25–9

Higgins, L. G. and Riley, N. D. *A Field Guide to the Butterflies of Britain and Europe* (1970). Every species is illustrated

Janus, H. *The Young Specialist Looks at Molluscs* (1965). A first-class guide to molluscs, fully illustrated with good keys and reasonably priced

Jones, A. W. and Castell, C. P. 'Some Notes on the Snails and Slugs of Devilsden Wood and the nearby Downs, Coulsdon', *London Naturalist*, 40 (1961), 131–6

Rundle, A. J. and Cooper, J. 'Some Recent Temporary Exposures of Clay in the London Area', *London Naturalist*, 49 (1970), 113–24

Simmons, J. W. 'Notes on the Occurrence of Holocene Shell Deposits at Chiswick Eyot', 43 (1964), 150–3

Wayside and Woodland Series (*The*) published by Warne includes some of the best guides to insects

Worms, C. G. M. de. 'The Moths of London and its Surroundings', *London Naturalist*, 37 (1957), 136–77

MAMMALS

Beames, Ian R. 'Bats in the London Area', *London Naturalist*, 43 (1964), 38–49

Burton, John A. 'The Distribution of Weasel, Stoat, Common Shrew, Roe Deer, Water Shrew and Mole in the London Area', *London Naturalist*, 45 (1966), 35–42

Corbet, G. B. *The Identification of British Mammals* (British Museum, Natural History, 1964). Has keys which help the beginner to identify mammals from skulls, as well as from the whole animal

Lawrence, M. J. and Brown, R. W. *Mammals of Britain, Their Tracks, Trails and Signs* (nd)

Morris, P. A. 'The Hedgehog in London', *London Naturalist*, 45 (1966), 43–50

Southern, H. N. (ed). *The Handbook of British Mammals* (1964). The most up-to-date and comprehensive treatment of the subject

Taylor-Page, F. J. (ed). *A Field Guide to British Deer* (1961). A useful little book covering more than the title might suggest

Teagle, W. G. 'The Harvest Mouse in the London Area', *London Naturalist*, 43 (1964), 136–49

Teagle, W. G. 'The Fox in the London Suburbs', *London Naturalist*, 46 (1967), 44–67

MAPS

Ordnance Survey, one inch to the mile cover London on sheets 160, 161, 170 and 171; there is also a single sheet of Greater London which embraces nearly all the area of these four maps. London is also covered by Ordnance Survey maps of $2\frac{1}{2}$ in to the mile and various other scales. Geological Survey, Land Utilisation and various other special maps are also available.

David & Charles also publish a reprint edition of the first one-inch Ordnance Survey.

Acknowledgements

I WOULD LIKE to thank all the many people who have supplied me with information, in particular members of the London Natural History Society. I have drawn freely on the society's journal the *London Naturalist*, as well as on various other journals. Any writer on the natural history of London owes a great debt to Richard Fitter's *London's Natural History* which, although written over a quarter of a century ago, is still one of the most useful sources of information. I have, of course, referred to many other books.

Of the many individuals who have given me help, special thanks are due to E. B. Bangerter, E. Groves and J. Laundon for help and advice on botanical matters; John Cooper for advice on the geology and mollusca; Tony Hutson for advice on entomology; Rod Alinson and Peter Grant for checking the recent records of birds; Brian Meadows for facts and figures concerning black redstarts; Dorothy Norman for locating some of the more obscure books and papers; K. Hyatt for help with the arachnids; W. G. Teagle for help and advice, particularly in my early days as an urban naturalist. I am grateful to Ron Hayward for drawing the diagrams; Margaret Whitbourne and Rosemary Rowson for typing the manuscript and finally Bruce Coleman, not only for helping with the photographs, but for first suggesting the book, many years ago.

Index

Without making the index completely unwieldy it has been impossible to give an entry for every animal, plant or place every time it is mentioned. Entries have been confined to general headings, except where a species or place is given more detailed treatment, or deserves special mention. Scientific names can be found in the text or in the appropriate checklist.

The detailed appendices and checklists (pp 121–60) have not been included in the index; in looking up animals, plants or places separate reference should be made to these lists.